THE JOURNEY

FROM WHO YOU ARE
TO WHO YOU'RE MEANT TO BE

Christina Vera & Maylin Sambois

The Journey: From Who You Are to Who You're Meant to Be
Copyright © 2025 by Christina Vera and Maylin Sambois

All rights reserved. No portion of this book may be reproduced, stored in a retrieval system, or transmitted in any form or by any means—electronic, mechanical, photocopy, recording, scanning, or other—except for brief quotations in critical reviews or articles, without the prior written permission of the publisher.

ISBN: 979-8-9994417-0-6 (Hardback)
ISBN: 979-8-9994417-1-3 (Paperback)
ISBN: 979-8-9994417-2-0 (Ebook)

TRUE PRINT FOR LIFE
https://trueprintforlife.com
For more information, contact
info@trueprintforlife.com

First Edition

Cover and interior design by Jonathan Lewis / Jonlin Creative

Printed in the United States of America

This book is dedicated to my family—Maritza, Julianna, Adrian, and Kent. Being your mother and wife is my greatest accomplishment, and I love you all more than words can ever express. My prayer for you has always been that you live boldly and create the life of your dreams—the life you so deeply deserve.

To my mother and siblings, my unwavering day-one supporters. You are the foundation of my strength and the inspiration behind my drive to create beyond my wildest dreams. Thank you for believing in me and fueling my journey.

~ **Christina**

To my son, Jireh: You are my greatest gift and answered prayer. Being your mother is my greatest joy. *Te amo para siempre.* God, I thank you!

To my parents, Luz and Tomas: Your resilience, strength, hard work, and wisdom have shaped the person I am. Thank you for lighting my way.

To my siblings: I am honored to be your older sister and to have your love and support. I am proud of how you all have embraced your own journeys!

To my stepparents: Being a stepparent is not easy. Thank you for contributing to my life and for all the lessons.

To my extended family and friends: You have loved, supported and given me so much. Each of you has been a special guide on my journey, and I am forever grateful.

~ **Maylin**

Table of Contents

INTRODUCTION: The Journey Begins 1

CHAPTER 1: My Current Self vs. My Future Self 7
CHAPTER 2: Clear the Air 23
CHAPTER 3: Planting The Seed 35
CHAPTER 4: Can Your No Mean No? 49
CHAPTER 5: The Power of Proximity 59
CHAPTER 6: Crossroads 77
CHAPTER 7: A Pathway to Progress 93
CHAPTER 8: Who Do You See in the Mirror? 109
CHAPTER 9: The Responsibility of Being Great 135
CHAPTER 10: The Journey Continues 153

Notes 165
About the Authors 167

INTRODUCTION

The Journey Begins

HAVE YOU EVER looked at your life—your choices, your patterns, your dreams—and thought, *There has to be more?*

We did too.

That quiet question lingered in our hearts through sleepless nights, business pivots, growing pains, and soul-stretching seasons of motherhood, friendship, and leadership. We were both building something—individually and together—but constantly found ourselves wrestling with the same frustrations: Why do we give so much but still feel stuck? Why is success sometimes so loud, but peace so quiet? And how do we stay rooted in purpose when life continues to pull us in so many directions?

The Journey was born from these very questions.

We are Christina and Maylin—best friends, mothers, entrepreneurs, and co-founders of a nonprofit organization that empowers girls and women to discover their voice, power, and purpose. In the midst of navigating family, business, loss, growth, and reinvention, we realized something essential: *No one has it all figured out.* But with the right tools, reflection, and support, you can begin to move with greater intention, deeper clarity, and bolder purpose.

This book is not about perfection—it's about *progress*.

Every chapter is a reflection of a lesson we've either learned or unlearned on our individual and shared paths. From learning how to set healthy boundaries, to healing generational wounds, to keeping promises to ourselves, this book invites you to reflect deeply, live freely, and grow forward.

We share the messy moments—the failures that humbled us, the no's that forced redirection, and the wins that tasted even sweeter because they were earned through grit and grace. We also share tools. Real ones. Not lofty advice, but actionable insights and mindset strategies that helped us reclaim our time, shift our perspectives, and show up as our fullest selves—again and again.

This book will challenge you, and with challenge often comes discomfort. But from that space, growth is born. While reading and participating in the writing and strategy exercises at the end of select chapters, remember to be open, honest, and kind to yourself.

To help you connect with our personal reflections throughout the book, you'll notice two icons used to represent our voices. When you see the **butterfly**, you're reading Maylin's perspective—a symbol of transformation, growth, and the beauty of becoming. When you see the **water**, you're hearing from Christina—a symbol of stillness, depth, and the power of renewal. We come from different walks, but our truths are rooted in the same soil: *resilience*, *hope*, and *purpose*.

One of our biggest growth moments thus far is understanding that failure doesn't define who you are or what you're capable of. Because it's been seen as undesirable, something to avoid, you must first reframe how you view it: as a teacher. Looking back on a failure reveals things you could have done differently. In that sense, each failure provides a blueprint—a guide on what to avoid or improve upon next time. Remember, tomorrow is a fresh start. Keep trying, and if that attempt doesn't work, try again. Letting fear or failure hold you back only keeps you stagnant.

The Journey Begins

As you step forward on this journey, open your mind and heart to see yourself as the warrior you truly are, flaws and all. We are all on a similar journey of self-discovery and fulfillment; what makes you unique is the individual path you take. How you've reached this moment may look different than how others have arrived at theirs, but that doesn't make your path any less significant. Own your journey, embrace it, and support others who are brave enough to journey toward their destinies too.

No matter where you were born, where you live, or your background, we all have a purpose. You have talents, visions, and gifts that are uniquely yours. Stop seeking validation from others for a vision or gift that was designed solely for you. It's not their job to understand or support it; it's your job to manifest it.

Do you have an inner drive that pulls you toward something more—not more in the material sense, but a deeper fulfillment? What is that restlessness you feel? These inner stirrings are often signs, signaling you to enhance your life and take things to the next level. Don't mistake that restlessness for mere insomnia that has led to countless sleepless nights. No, that unease comes from your soul. It is trying to awaken you! Believe us! That's how this book was written! You can't sleep because you know it's time to start writing that play, refining that business idea, or going back to school. In the quiet hours, you think, *Do I have what it takes?*

The Journey: From Who You Are to Who You're Meant to Be will guide you in building strategies, shifting your mindset, becoming self-aware, and creating routines centered around your mental and physical well-being. Nothing you create or pursue can succeed if you aren't mentally and physically strong. Like anything you aspire to, your well-being requires continuous effort. You didn't become a teacher, an artist, or an expert overnight. It took practice, study, research, and commitment. Yet so many of us put our physical and mental health at the bottom of our to-do list. While reading and participating in the writing and strategy exercises at the end of each chapter, remember to be open, honest, and kind to yourself.

Through this journey, you'll discover how to:

- Confront the disconnect between your current self and who you're becoming
- Clear space emotionally and mentally to make room for purpose
- Plant new seeds of thought and discipline that align with your values
- Create boundaries that honor your peace and your calling
- Reframe negative thoughts and hard seasons as teachers
- Build daily habits that reinforce your bigger vision
- Move beyond fear, shame, or perfectionism into self-trust and progress
- Keep showing up for *you*, even when the road gets hard

By the end of this journey, our hope is that you'll walk away not just inspired—but equipped. With more confidence. More clarity. More courage to show up for the life you deserve.

———————————— ————————————

I wish I could tell you that this journey will be smooth and picture-perfect, but the truth is, perfection doesn't exist—not in the way we often imagine. Let go of the idea that perfection is something real or achievable. Instead, embrace progress. Each day, whether it's a great day or one you'd rather do over, remember that it's not about getting everything right. It's about moving forward.

Be kind to yourself. A tough day does not define your entire life. You are needed, valued, and seen. Recognizing who you truly

The Journey Begins

are also means understanding who you are not. So don't make permanent decisions based on temporary relationships or fleeting circumstances. Take risks, knowing that even if things don't go as planned, it's not failure if you're learning and growing from it. When you don't succeed at something, ask, "What did I learn from this experience?"

In a world of unknowns and challenges, be the light others can depend on. This is your time. You deserve this, and you owe it to yourself to dig deep and become the best version of who you're meant to be.

Let this book be your companion on your own journey—a gentle reminder that you are never alone, and your transformation is already in motion.

Pause. Reflect. Reimagine. React. Reclaim.

Because the life you're dreaming of? It's already within you.

As women, nurturers, leaders, and dreamers, we often find ourselves pouring into everyone else—our families, our communities, our work. But true transformation begins when we also pour into ourselves. This book is your reminder that you must become your own priority. When you give yourself permission to slow down, reconnect, and reflect, you begin to rediscover the divine gifts that were placed inside of you long before the world told you to hustle, hide, or play small.

During a Millionaire Mastermind conversation, something Dave Gambrill shared struck me so deeply that it became a mantra I now carry on the hard days. He said, "*I would be doing a disservice to my God if I didn't go all-out with the gifts He has given me.*" Whew! That landed in my spirit like a divine assignment. And I don't know about you, but I refuse to play it safe or shrink back. So I ask you, what mantra, affirmation, or belief do *you* need to repeat

THE JOURNEY

when your journey feels heavy or uncertain? This book is filled with stories, tools, and strategies to help you keep going—and go all out, boldly, in the direction of your calling.

Let the journey begin!

◆ Christina
🦋 Maylin

CHAPTER 1

My Current Self vs. My Future Self

Your future self is not a stranger. She is you, evolved. And every choice you make today is either getting you closer to her—or further away. Don't stay trapped on the endless carousel of your past.

—CHRISTINA VERA

AS WE BEGIN the internal work of shifting mindsets, it's essential to establish agreements. These agreements serve as the foundation for building or enhancing systems that are healthy, supportive, and accountable. Take a moment and ask yourself: *Who am I right now, and is this who I want to be?*

This is not a question of shame or judgment. It's an invitation. A mirror. A pause in the busyness of life to look inward and ask, *Where am I? What's working? What's not working?* And more importantly: *What am I willing to change to become the version of me I haven't met yet?*

This chapter marks the beginning of *The Journey*—not just our journey, but yours too. And like any meaningful journey, it starts with *honesty*.

Sonia Sotomayor, associate justice of the U.S. Supreme Court, said, "It is important for all of us to appreciate where we come from and how that history has really shaped us in ways that we might not understand."[1] At the stage of life many of us are in now, this quote takes on a whole new meaning. By "stage of life," we acknowledge that we have made space in our minds and spirits to receive and process insights that can guide us toward forgiveness, peace, and—above all—understanding.

Before you can build the life you want, you must evaluate the life you're currently living. Too often we chase the idea of "better" without ever asking what better means to *us*. We adopt society's definitions of success, beauty, strength, or achievement without ever slowing down to ask ourselves: *Is this even aligned with what I value?*

Taking inventory of your current self is an act of bravery. It requires you to acknowledge what's working—and confront what's not. It asks you to face the habits, fears, thought patterns, and relationships that may be keeping you small, stagnant, or unfulfilled. But this isn't about tearing yourself down—it's about creating *awareness*. And awareness is where transformation begins.

Because if you don't know where you *are*, how can you ever map out where you're going?

The intention of this chapter is to help you reset—your mindset, your emotions, and the way you show up in the world. Give yourself permission to extend grace, embrace stillness, and be fully present in this moment. Release the weight of past mistakes and limiting beliefs. Today is a fresh start—a blank canvas, waiting for you to envision and create the future you truly desire.

Between your current self and your future self is a gap. That gap is filled with choices, habits, beliefs, and daily decisions. It's the

My Current Self vs. My Future Self

space where growth happens, or doesn't. If we don't consciously fill that space with intention, we run the risk of living on autopilot, drifting, reacting, and repeating patterns that don't serve the woman, leader, or purpose-driven soul we're trying to become.

Visualizing your future self isn't just about lofty dreams; it's about clarity. It's about asking: *What kind of life do I want to live? What kind of impact do I want to make? How do I want to feel when I wake up each day?*

Now imagine her—your future self. She's you, but wiser. Freer. More rooted. She's moved through pain but carries peace. She honors her boundaries. She moves with purpose, not pressure. She doesn't second-guess her worth. She remembers who she is even when the world forgets.

She exists. But she's waiting for you to meet her.

As you progress, you'll encounter prompts in this book to Pause, Reflect, and React (PRR). In these moments, take time to do just that. "React" here means journaling your thoughts, feelings, insights, and lightbulb moments. We encourage you to capture these raw reflections in a journal or the notes app on your phone. Some PRR moments will include guided questions to help you explore and expand on your thoughts.

Leading a more intentional, healthy life doesn't mean life's challenges will suddenly stop; in fact, they may intensify. Therefore, it's crucial to be clear about what you want in life both personally and professionally and to establish core values around it. Just as companies have mission or vision statements as their North Star, you, too, should reflect on how each decision aligns with your core values and your "why." This practice ensures that your actions remain true to your purpose and goals.

In your journey toward creating a fulfilling life and pursuing the career you desire and deserve, one of the pivotal steps is identifying and aligning with your core values. These values are the compass that guides your behavior, mindset, and strategic decisions. They are the foundation upon which you can build a life and career that truly resonates with your authentic self.

When you are clear about your values, you gain clarity about what matters most—what you're willing to say "yes" to, and just as importantly, what you're no longer available to tolerate. Core values serve as a filter, helping you navigate opportunities, relationships, and challenges with greater confidence and alignment. They become your personal blueprint, allowing you to lead from a place of purpose rather than pressure, and to move through life not simply chasing success, but defining it on your own terms.

Whether you're deciding which role to step into, how to spend your time, or what legacy you want to leave, your values act as the steady ground beneath your feet. And when external circumstances shift—as they often do—it's your internal compass that will keep you rooted, resilient, and ready to rise.

Growth isn't about becoming someone *else*—it's about *remembering* who you are at your core and choosing to become her, on purpose, day by day. So how do we begin closing the space between who we are and who we're meant to become? It starts with honest reflection and intention.

In this next section, grab something to write with or open a fresh page in your journal—you'll want to have a dedicated space to Pause, Reflect, and React (PRR). This isn't just a reading exercise—it's an invitation to slow down, be honest with yourself, and actively engage in your growth process.

As mentioned earlier, the PRR method is designed to help you connect more deeply with the content and, more importantly, with yourself. When you *pause*, you give yourself permission to breathe and center. When you *reflect*, you begin to notice patterns, emotions, and beliefs that may have been operating silently in the background of your life. And when you *react*, that's your opportunity to write freely—capturing your thoughts, feelings, moments of clarity, and even the questions that still linger.

This is your safe space. There are no right or wrong answers here—just truth. And the more honest you are with yourself in this process, the more powerful your transformation will be. So take your time, be gentle, and let your own words guide you forward. Growth doesn't come from reading alone—it comes from *doing the inner work.*

WHY ARE CORE VALUES ESSENTIAL?

Core values are essential because they serve as the internal framework that shapes how we live, lead, and make decisions. In a world full of distractions, expectations, and shifting priorities, your values anchor you to what truly matters. They help you move with intention rather than impulse, and make choices that reflect who you are—not just what others expect you to be. When your life and career are aligned with your core values, you experience greater clarity, confidence, and peace. You begin to attract opportunities, relationships, and environments that support your growth rather than compromise it. Without clearly defined values, it's easy to drift, settle, or sacrifice your authenticity. But when you lead with your values, you lead with purpose—and that is the foundation of a life that feels fulfilling, empowered, and fully your own.

Clarity and Direction: Your core values are the guiding principles that define what is most important to you. They act as a compass, providing clarity and direction in your decision-making process. When you align your actions with your values, you naturally move toward a life and career that are in harmony with your true self.

Authenticity: Living in accordance with your core values allows you to be authentic. It means being true to yourself and not trying to fit into someone else's mold or expectations. This authenticity resonates with others and can lead to more meaningful connections and relationships, both personally and professionally.

Motivation and Fulfillment: When your actions align with your values, you feel a deep sense of motivation and fulfillment. Tasks that are in line with your values are more engaging and satisfying. This motivation can be a powerful driver for success in both your personal and professional endeavors.

Resilience: Knowing your core values can also help you weather life's challenges more effectively. When faced with difficult decisions or setbacks, your values can provide a strong foundation to bounce back and stay on course.

Decision-Making: Identifying your core values simplifies decision-making. It becomes easier to weigh options and choose the path that aligns with what matters most to you. This can save you from the stress and regret that often accompany decisions made without a clear understanding of your values.

TEST YOUR VALUES

As you go through life, test your values in various situations. Do they consistently guide your decisions and actions? Are there any values that no longer resonate with you? Your values may evolve over time, so it's important to periodically reassess them.

In the pursuit of creating the life, career, and business you desire, understanding and embracing your core values will serve as a compass, helping you navigate the many choices and challenges you'll encounter along the way. In the chapters ahead, we will explore how to leverage your values to shift your behavior, mindset, and strategy effectively, enabling you to craft a life and business that align with your deepest aspirations and desires.

My Current Self vs. My Future Self

Christina (C) & Maylin (M) sample of nonnegotiables and prioritization of personal values.

No meetings before nine a.m., as it is a priority for me to drop off my kids at school in the mornings without interruption.

My first thirty minutes of the day are dedicated to God (prayer), writing my gratitude list, and practicing being still. It's important for me to center my heart and mind first thing in the morning. I don't know what the day will bring, but doing this helps me navigate any unplanned/planned life challenges!

Reflecting on these questions—and answering them with honesty—is essential for more than one reason. Let us take a moment to explain the deeper purpose behind this process. When we look up a company or organization, we typically go straight to their mission statement: What do they stand for? Who do they support? But what if someone asked you for your *personal mission statement*? Would you have an answer ready?

Think about it this way: We often read reviews of products or restaurants, relying on others' experiences to guide our decisions. Now imagine if there were a "review history" capturing what others would say about their experiences working with you, dating you, hiring you, and so on. How would those experiences be detailed?

It's essential to show up consistently with your core values shining throughout everything you do. Your values can't be hidden in the background; they should be evident in both light and challenging moments. Not everyone lives this way. We've all encountered people who are unpredictable in relationships or work environments. But taking the time to reassess your own values can help you evaluate how you show up, how you conduct business, and with whom you choose to work.

It's also crucial to be mindful of your spending power. One of the privileges of democracy is choice. You can choose to invest in, purchase from, and collaborate with companies and individuals whose values align with your own. Admittedly, in life and business, things aren't always so simple. Sometimes we have to work with people who challenge us, and that's part of life. Yet while you may not always have control over *who* you work with, you do control *how* you engage with them. We've all heard the phrase, "Don't let people take you out of character." It's simple advice but often one of the hardest directives to live by.

Growing up, I learned to be on the defensive. It was how I protected myself in a world that didn't always feel safe. And while I don't seek out conflict, I've always been prepared to stand my ground when necessary. Over time, I've come to understand my defensiveness was instinctual—but not always helpful. Reacting out of habit isn't the same as responding from a place of clarity.

As I've grown, I've learned that when I can quiet my mind and regulate my emotions, something deeper emerges: *discernment*. Discernment has become one of my most trusted inner guides. It allows me to assess people, situations, and opportunities with wisdom rather than reactivity. And every time I've ignored that inner voice, I've ended up paying for it—emotionally, professionally, or spiritually.

Discernment, I've found, is closely tied to values. It's the tool that helps you test whether your actions reflect what you *say* you believe. And here's the truth: If you never pause to test your values in real-life scenarios, they remain unproven theories—nice to profess but hard to live. It's in the tension of leadership, the chaos of motherhood, the exhaustion of entrepreneurship, and the frustration of workplace politics that your values either hold firm or fall apart.

Values aren't just words; they are *anchors*. They keep you grounded when everything around you feels uncertain. But values can also evolve. As you grow, you may find that some values no longer resonate, or that others rise in importance based on your season of life.

When I began my professional journey, I didn't yet know how to articulate my core values. I just knew what felt right—and what didn't. Maylin and I entered the workforce fifteen years ago, bright-eyed and ambitious. But nothing prepared us for the emotional weight of navigating environments filled with cliques, unhealed leaders, and competitive, scarcity-driven mindsets. We were told how to build careers but not how to protect our *sense of self* within them.

Eventually, we hit a crossroads: continue to survive systems that were draining us, or redefine what success looked like on our own terms. That's when our values became our compass. We had to ask hard questions:

- Is this environment aligned with my integrity?
- Do I feel safe to be myself here?
- Am I sacrificing peace for a paycheck?
- Is my work meaningful or merely tolerable?

Those questions weren't always easy to answer. And the answers didn't always lead to immediate change. But they did lead to *clarity*.

It's also important to stay grounded in reality. While it's empowering to follow your dreams, the "just quit your job and be your own boss" narrative can feel like a fantasy if it ignores financial realities. I've experienced both—working in systems and building my own. And the truth? I've worked longer hours and faced more uncertainty as an entrepreneur than I ever did as an employee. But I also feel more aligned because my values are driving the vision.

There is no shame in working for someone else while building your dream. And there's no shame in *only* working for someone else. Every role matters. What matters most is that *you're not betraying your values to stay in rooms you've outgrown.*

If you're currently in a role that feels misaligned, don't discount it. Every job, every uncomfortable moment, every seemingly meaningless task is teaching you something—either what you're here to create or what you're meant to change. Think of each role as a testing ground not just for your skills, but for your values.

Write down your core values. Post them where you can see them. Let them guide how you respond to conflict, how you lead your team, how you design your days, and how you make decisions. And revisit them often. Ask: *Are these values still true for me? Are they showing up in my life? Or are they just words on a wall?*

Because every decision you make—whether in your relationships, your business, or your personal growth—either moves you closer to your values or pulls you away from them. That's why it's not enough to just name your values—you have to *live* them, test them, and sometimes wrestle with them.

Real alignment is forged in the everyday moments when you're forced to choose between what's easy and what's right, between what pleases others and what honors your truth. And when those values are tested—as they inevitably will be—don't see it as failure. See it as refinement. Every challenge, every misstep, and every hard decision is an opportunity to come back stronger, clearer, and more committed to the person you're becoming. Let the testing clarify who you are—not define who you think you have to be.

DISCOVERING YOUR WHY: THE FUEL FOR LIFE'S PURPOSE

In your pursuit of a more fulfilling and purpose-driven life, one of the most crucial steps is to identify your why or your purpose. Your why is the underlying reason that propels you forward, gives meaning to your actions, and provides a deep sense of fulfillment. It serves as the driving force behind your behavior, mindset, and strategic decisions. Discovering your why can also be a catalyst for transformative change.

As I embarked on this next chapter of my journey, I realized how easy it had been to get swept up in the daily grind—checking off to-do lists, juggling responsibilities, and chasing success without ever stopping to ask myself why I started in the first place. That's when I revisited Dean Graziosi's 7 Levels Deep Exercise, and everything shifted.[2] I had explored the surface of my why before, but this time I was determined to go deeper. Layer by layer, I peeled back the motivations I thought were driving me, only to uncover a more powerful emotional truth at my core. It was transformative. What made the experience even more special was doing it alongside Christina—sharing that level of vulnerability and reflection with someone who understands the journey was empowering. I encourage you to give yourself that same gift of clarity. You'll find the link to Dean's template in our resource guide. Take your time with it, be honest, and get ready to be surprised by what you discover. Let's explore ways it can transform your life.

THE POWER OF KNOWING YOUR WHY

Your why acts as a guiding star, offering clarity and direction in a world that can often feel chaotic or overwhelming. With a clear why, you are better equipped to make decisions that align with your values and long-term goals. This clarity allows your purpose to become the foundation for your choices. Rather than questioning every decision, you start making choices that align with your vision for the future.

When your path is illuminated by a deep sense of purpose, you can navigate life's complexities with a steady sense of direction. This inner clarity not only simplifies decision-making but also strengthens your confidence in pursuing your dreams.

Motivation and Resilience: A strong why provides the fuel to keep going, even when you encounter setbacks or challenges. When life gets difficult, it's easy to feel discouraged, but a clear sense of purpose can rekindle your motivation. Knowing why you're pursuing a particular goal creates resilience, allowing you to face obstacles with a tenacity that's hard to shake.

Think of athletes, artists, or leaders who have faced rejection or failure. What kept them going wasn't necessarily the desire for fame or recognition, but a deep, internal purpose that made the struggle worth it. Your why is the powerful motivator that helps you get back up when you fall, reminding you that the journey, no matter how challenging, is worthwhile.

Alignment with Values: Your why is deeply intertwined with your core values, making it a powerful force in shaping your actions and decisions. When you understand and embrace your purpose, you begin to live in alignment with your authentic self. This alignment fosters a sense of integrity because your actions are consistently aligned with your beliefs.

Living according to your values brings a sense of wholeness and authenticity. It means that you're not just going through the motions or following external expectations—you're living from a place of truth. In a world where it's easy to lose ourselves in the noise, knowing your why keeps you grounded, reminding you to stay true to what matters most.

Passion and Fulfillment: Understanding your why can ignite a passionate pursuit of your goals. When you're driven by a genuine purpose, your actions feel meaningful, and this sense of meaning is deeply fulfilling. Passion, after all, comes from doing work that resonates with your why. You find yourself energized and motivated not only by the results you achieve, but also by the process of working toward something you care about.

This fulfillment spills into all areas of your life, creating a sense of harmony between your personal and professional worlds. When your daily efforts align with your deeper purpose, the work becomes a source of joy and satisfaction, not just a means to an end. This is why so many people say that finding purpose in your work can feel like "never working a day in your life."

Impact and Contribution: A meaningful why often extends beyond personal satisfaction to include a positive impact on others. Your purpose is often linked to making a difference in the world, whether by improving someone's life, contributing to your community, or advancing a cause you believe in. This desire to contribute creates a sense of fulfillment that goes beyond individual achievements; it's about leaving a legacy.

Knowing your why can be the catalyst for creating change, however big or small. When your actions contribute to a greater good, you feel a profound sense of connection and significance. This sense of purpose not only enriches your life but also has the potential to inspire and uplift those around you.

PUTTING IT ALL TOGETHER: LIVING YOUR WHY DAILY

Understanding your why isn't a one-time discovery; it's a commitment to live with intentionality. To get started, take time to reflect on what truly matters to you. Ask yourself: "What drives me? What values are nonnegotiable? How do I want to contribute to the world?" Write these reflections down as a personal mission statement, a reminder of your purpose.

THE JOURNEY

Once you have a clearer sense of your why, find ways to integrate it into your everyday actions. Align your daily choices with your purpose, set goals that reflect your values, and build resilience by revisiting your why during difficult times. Over time, you'll notice that your sense of purpose strengthens your confidence, increases your fulfillment, and allows you to live a life that feels deeply rewarding.

Embracing your why is the first step toward a life of clarity, resilience, and meaningful impact. When you live with purpose, every challenge, achievement, and decision hold greater meaning. The power of knowing your why transforms not just what you do, but how you experience your journey.

                                                                                                      ◊ Christina
                                                                                                        ✤ Maylin

PAUSE, REFLECT, AND REACT

Test Your Values

Use the prompts at the end of each chapter to reflect on your core values and how they show up in your life today.

REFLECT
- When have you felt most fulfilled or proud?
- What areas of your life feel aligned? What feels off?
- Where do you feel most alive? Where do you feel stuck?
- What were you doing in those meaningful moments?

VISION CASTING
Write a letter from your *future self* to your *current self*:
- What has she overcome?
- What did she let go of?
- How does she carry herself now?

TAKE ACTION
- What's *one small thing* you can do this week to honor your future self?
    - » A boundary to set:
    - » A decision to follow through on:
    - » An affirmation to repeat:

ROLE MODELS
- Who do you admire, and why?
- What values do they live by that you also want to embody?

VALUES CHECK

- Make a list of values that resonate with you (e.g., integrity, creativity, peace, freedom).
- Highlight your *nonnegotiables*. These are your core values.
- Keep them visible and revisit them often.

CHAPTER 2

Clear the Air

Keep your thoughts positive, because your thoughts become your words. Keep your words positive, because your behaviors become your habits. Keep your habits positive, because your habits become your values. Keep your values positive, because your values become your destiny.

—GANDHI

BEFORE YOU CAN move forward, you have to be willing to *release*. That release might be emotional. It might be mental. Sometimes it's even spiritual. But in every case, it begins with the decision to *clear the air*—to stop carrying what was never meant to come with you into your next season.

Clearing the air is not just a metaphor; it's a necessary action that takes many forms in real life. Emotionally, it might mean forgiving someone who never apologized, extending grace to yourself, or finally letting go of long-held shame. Mentally, it can look like challenging negative self-talk, breaking free from limiting beliefs, or putting an end to the exhausting cycle of overthinking.

Relationally, it could involve having that hard conversation you've been avoiding, setting boundaries that protect your peace, or creating distance from toxic dynamics. Spiritually, clearing the air may require you to reconnect with your faith, engage in grounding practices, or surrender the need to control outcomes. Whatever form it takes, the act of clearing the air opens the door to clarity, healing, and forward movement.

Clearing the air isn't about pretending the past didn't happen. It's not about suppressing pain or skipping over hard experiences. In fact, it's quite the opposite. It's about *acknowledging* what was, *accepting* what is, and *choosing* what will be. It's about making peace with your story so you can stop reliving it—and start rewriting it.

Sometimes we hold onto the past not because we miss it, but because we're still angry with what happened. We resent the people who hurt us, the time we lost, the things that didn't go as planned. And that resentment builds like fog, clouding our vision and dimming our hope.

But what if instead of resenting your past, you *thanked* it?

What if you took a moment to say, "That hurt, but it taught me something." What if you recognized that your past, as complicated as it may be, helped shape the strength, clarity, and wisdom you carry now?

We've learned firsthand that gratitude is one of the most powerful tools for release. When you can look back and extract the lesson—even from the pain—you begin to set yourself free. Free to grow. Free to evolve. Free to make decisions that aren't rooted in wounds but in wisdom.

This chapter is your invitation to pause and reflect. To breathe deep and be honest about what you've been holding onto. It's your moment to clear the air—not just with others but with yourself. Because the future you want can't be built on the weight of what you haven't let go of.

Clear the Air

To move forward, you must be willing to release the past. This doesn't mean forgetting it, as there's wisdom in acknowledging history. Sometimes you can't release the past because you are resentful of it. Taking a moment to thank your past for the lessons it brought and for helping you to arrive at this moment is essential to your growth.

There was a season in my life when I held onto resentment like it was armor. I thought I was protecting myself—shielding my heart from more hurt. But in reality, I was only blocking my own blessings and robbing myself of peace. I carried the weight of childhood trauma for years, and I didn't fully understand how deeply those early wounds had embedded themselves into my mindset, my self-worth, and my spirit. The fear, the anger, the silence—it all became part of my internal dialogue. And because I never gave those feelings space to breathe or be healed, they followed me into adulthood.

Later, in business and leadership, I encountered situations that reopened those wounds—people who betrayed me, misused my trust, or spoke against me. For years, just hearing their names or seeing their faces would trigger something in me. My whole energy would shift. I'd smile through it, but inside, I was unsettled. That's when I realized I was still giving them power—over my mood, my day, my thoughts. And the cost was too high.

So I made a choice. I chose forgiveness—not for *them* but for *me*. I reminded myself that the greatest revenge wasn't bitterness or retaliation; it was peace. It was purpose. It was waking up every day, doing right by others, and building something beautiful in spite of what I'd endured. I didn't need to prove anything. I just needed to keep going.

It's so easy to sit in pain, sorrow, or even the desire for

revenge. But the truth is, every painful encounter—whether it occurred in childhood or adulthood—has shaped your testimony. It's not who you are, but it *is* part of your story. And at some point, you must decide to no longer carry what doesn't belong to your next chapter.

So pray for it. Pray through it. Pray for *them*. And then release your feelings. Because your peace is too precious to trade for someone else's offense.

Manifestation begins with *clearing space*. Just like you can't pour into a cup that's already full, you can't manifest the life you truly desire while holding onto resentment, fear, or limiting beliefs. When you *clear the air*—mentally, emotionally, and spiritually—you make room for new energy, new possibilities, and new direction. Manifestation isn't just about vision boards or affirmations—it's about alignment. It's about becoming emotionally and energetically available for what you say you want. Releasing the past, forgiving yourself, and letting go of what no longer serves you is what opens the pathway for your future self to emerge. Only then can you call in blessings from a place of clarity, not chaos.

The energy you put into the world—through your thoughts, words, and intentions—has the power to shape outcomes, both positive and negative. That's why it's so important to speak life, remain mindful of your mindset, and be intentional about what you declare over yourself and others. When you are unable to express your emotions or deal with life's setbacks, you often internalize that pain, letting it build up until you become overwhelmed with frustration. At this point, you may become stagnant, bitter, and a source of negativity for others. In this state, it's difficult to see potential, promise, or favor; instead, you remain in a place of familiarity and control, often perceiving yourself as a victim. Over time, you become accustomed to rejection and pain, embracing suffering as if it's normal.

Clear the Air

Clearing the air also means releasing the illusion of control. One of the hardest lessons to learn is that you cannot control how others show up, how they respond, or whether they apologize or acknowledge the harm they've caused. But what you *can* control is what you carry. You get to choose what stays in your spirit, what takes up space in your mind, and how you move forward. That choice is where your power lives. When you stop trying to manage or fix what's beyond your control, you create space—space for clarity, space for healing, and most importantly, space for peace. Because when we truly clear the air, we don't just release old weight—we make room for something greater. Peace is the quiet reward that follows release. It's not just a feeling; it's the result of intentionally letting go of what no longer belongs.

Many of our (Christina's and Maylin's) actions in the past helped us survive the journey, and now we know that these actions served a purpose: survival. Now that we have thanked our past, we get to decide how we want to live our present and future. But understanding why we think or react in specific ways often leads back to past experiences. If your goal is to adopt a new mindset, lifestyle, or way of doing business, it's essential to trace the roots of your current perspectives and habits to rewire them for the future. Often, anxiety lingers because we haven't fully processed the past or asked for help. Seeking support—whether from friends, mentors, or a licensed professional—isn't a sign of weakness; it's a powerful step toward clarity and growth.

Therapy is for everyone, regardless of circumstance. Consulting a mental health professional regularly, even just for a fresh, nonjudgmental perspective, can be invaluable for dealing with challenges in life, business, and relationships. Many insurance plans cover therapy sessions at little to no cost, and resources like www.psychologytoday.com can connect you with support services, and some are free. Knowing how to process, reset, and respond to life's events is key to nurturing healthy relationships with others and, most importantly, with yourself.

When we haven't taken preventive steps to protect our mental health, it can be challenging to distinguish between what is real and what is simply fear. Old fears can resurface when new situations remind us of past pain, leading us to expect the worst and, ultimately, halting our growth. Remember, while our past shapes our mindset, we have the power to redefine our narrative. Many of the fears we harbor are unlikely to come true, yet we allow them to disrupt our present. Changing our reality begins with changing our thoughts.

Here's a tip to help with this transformation: When assessing an opportunity, relationship, or decision, notice the types of questions you're asking yourself. Your mindset in that moment heavily influences how you evaluate and proceed. Emotional intelligence plays a significant role here, so study it, apply it, and explore resources to develop it. Today, we have access to countless resources (from online videos and courses to in-person workshops) that can guide us in this journey. Find the link to resources at the end of this book to help you transform your thoughts and be more present in the moment.

As you begin to shift your inner narrative by reframing your resentment and creating mental space and understanding, you'll find yourself making decisions based on facts and principles rather than subconscious fears. Dr. Myles Monroe once highlighted the power of self-manifestation, saying, "Discontent is the seed to change. You will never change what you tolerate."[1] To truly become who you were meant to be, you must let go of tolerance for what no longer serves you and step into a mindset of transformation and growth.

Resentment is a slow-burning weight we often carry without realizing how heavy it truly is. It shows up subtly—through our silence, through the way we shrink in certain spaces, or how our hearts race when a name is mentioned. It feels like self-protection, but more often than not, it's self-sabotage. When you hold onto resentment, your focus is anchored to the past. Your emotional energy is tied to moments you were meant to grow *through*—not live *in*. And the longer you hold on, the harder it becomes to see the possibilities in front of you.

You can't fully step into your next season if your energy is still tied to someone who hurt you in the last season. You can't claim your peace while clutching tightly to pain. And you can't walk in freedom while dragging the chains of what should have been. The truth is, resentment clouds your vision. It keeps you reactive instead of intentional. It can trick you into thinking you're being strong when in reality, you are stuck.

But here's the reframe: What if you stopped viewing that painful moment as something that broke you and instead saw it as something that *built you*? What if instead of replaying what they did to you, you started reflecting on how far you've come since? That shift in perspective won't happen overnight, but it begins with the decision to see yourself not as a victim of your past, but as the author of your next chapter. Releasing resentment doesn't mean pretending the hurt didn't happen. It means refusing to let it control what happens *next*. Freeing yourself from resentment is not about excusing what someone did but reclaiming your energy, your peace, and your power.

So ask yourself: Who or what am I still giving power to? What would it feel like to finally let that go? And then—when you're ready—*do it*. Not for them. For *you*.

EAGLE TALK

A mindset shift for those ready to rise.

To truly become who you were meant to be, you must release your tolerance for things that no longer serve your growth.

THE JOURNEY

Transformation begins the moment you choose to stop settling and start soaring.

You may have heard of the eagle mindset, and it's more than a metaphor. Eagles were created to rise. They soar high above storms, only coming down to rest, eat, or raise the next generation. Their vision is sharp. Their instincts strong. They don't concern themselves with chickens or peacocks because those birds weren't designed to fly like they were.

Chickens stay grounded not because they're weak, but because they know their role. Peacocks are beautiful, but their gift is to display, not to ascend.

The point is: *Not everyone is meant to fly in the same way.* But when you are an eagle trying to live like a chicken—or forcing someone else to play a role they weren't built for—everyone loses.

Your mindset, your placement, and your purpose are all connected. To rise, you must understand:

- Your **gift**
- Your **purpose**
- Your **role**
- Your **responsibility**

Stop caging your potential. Stop clinging to environments that clip your wings. Stop trying to "make it work" when everything in your spirit is telling you to rise.

An eagle mindset is a commitment to self-awareness, alignment, and elevation.

Know who you are and then act accordingly.

--- ---

Clearing the air can be different for you. Maybe you need to let go of that story that's holding you back, or letting go of habits that no longer serve you. It could also be about speaking your voice and standing for what you believe. I used to believe that staying quiet was the high road. That if I stayed silent, I was keeping the peace. But over time, I realized I was just avoiding the storm. A storm that was already brewing inside me.

I've smiled through pain. I've nodded in rooms where my truth was silenced. I've swallowed words that could've set me free, just to keep others comfortable. And what did it cost me? My peace. My clarity. My voice.

"Clearing the air" used to terrify me. I feared rejection, misunderstanding, or being labeled as "too much." But the real weight wasn't in the confrontation—it was in the suppression. The more I buried, the heavier I felt. I became a version of myself that wasn't whole.

It wasn't until I sat with my silence and asked, "Who am I protecting?" that I realized, I had abandoned myself too many times in the name of false harmony. Now, I choose differently.

I no longer confuse peacekeeping with peacebuilding. One avoids the fire. The other transforms it. Speaking my truth with love is my act of self-respect. And when I clear the air, I do it not just for others, but for the little girl in me who once felt unseen and unheard.

This isn't about being right. It's about being real. It's about releasing the tension that lives in the unsaid. It's about honoring both my voice and the connection it seeks. Clearing the air isn't always easy but neither is suffocating in silence. I've learned that the peace I desire begins with me. And sometimes, the most courageous thing we can do is speak—even if our voice shakes.

And now, I release the resentment that's lingered like a shadow. Not because it didn't hurt, but because I'm ready to heal. I'm ready to stop carrying what was never mine to hold. I forgive not to excuse but to unburden. To make room for the light to enter. I move forward, even if my steps are shaky. Even if I can't see the whole path. I trust that choosing love over fear even for myself is the most radical act of freedom.

Clearing the air is about softening. Releasing. Rising. It's about making peace with the past so I can walk fully into the present.

◆ Christina
✹ Maylin

PAUSE, REFLECT, AND REACT

Shifting the Inner Narrative

Is there truly a lesson in everything? Not every lesson is pleasant, and at times these experiences can be traumatic. In these cases, we strongly suggest the support of a mental health expert to support you in navigating this experience. Exploring perception, perspective, and reality can reveal valuable insights, especially when faced with challenges. How we interpret our experiences can be a powerful choice. Making the conscious effort to see opportunity in the face of opposition is a practice that builds resilience.

1. What stories have I been telling myself that no longer serve me? ("I'm not ready." "I always mess things up." "I have to do it alone.") Where did these beliefs come from, and are they even true?
2. What fears do I often allow to guide my decisions? How might my life shift if I made decisions based on values and truth rather than fear?
3. What emotional clutter am I holding onto that's taking up space in my mind and spirit? Resentment? Guilt? Perfectionism? Comparison?
4. What does "clearing the air" look like for me in this season? Is it a conversation I need to have, a boundary I need to set, or a limiting belief I need to release?
5. When was the last time I trusted myself fully? What would it look like to start doing that again?
6. What does my most grounded, present, and emotionally available self think about my current situation? How does her perspective differ from the fearful or reactive version of me?

7. What are the core principles or values I want guiding my life moving forward? How can I align my decisions with those values?
8. How do I want to *feel* in my next chapter? What do I need to release to make room for that feeling?

Once you've acknowledged what's been weighing you down, the next step is to intentionally speak life into your present and your future. Affirmations are more than feel-good quotes. They are daily declarations of who you are becoming and what you are choosing to believe. The words we speak have power, and when spoken consistently, they begin to reshape the narratives we hold about ourselves and our lives.

Speak these affirmations aloud. Write them down. Post them somewhere you'll see them daily. Let them serve as reminders that you are no longer defined by what you've been through. You are shaped by what you choose to rise into.

Repeat after me:

- *I release what no longer serves me.*
- *I make peace with my past and create space for my future.*
- *I am no longer bound by fear, shame, or guilt.*
- *I choose clarity, peace, and freedom in this new chapter.*

Take a deep breath. These words are yours now. Let them settle in your heart and guide your next step forward.

CHAPTER 3

Planting The Seed

The best time to plant a tree was twenty years ago. The second-best time is now.
—CHINESE PROVERB

SEEDS WERE PLANTED in you long before you ever knew what they meant. Some were planted in moments of joy—when someone believed in you, encouraged you, or saw your potential before you saw it in yourself. Others were planted in pain—in the silence of being misunderstood, in the struggle of being overlooked, or in the ache of not having your needs fully met. These experiences—whether nurturing or challenging—became the soil, sun, and rain of your becoming. And like all seeds, they didn't always grow visibly right away. But they *did* take root.

These early seeds began shaping your inner world—your values, your fears, your sense of self, your coping mechanisms, your capacity for love, trust, and resilience. Even now, they influence the way you respond to opportunities, the way you carry your ambition, the way you set (or avoid) boundaries. They are foundational, but they are not final.

As you continue on the journey of personal growth, it's natural to want to "figure it all out." To look outward for signs, answers, mentors, or even permission to begin again. We search podcasts, books, social media, or relationships hoping they'll provide the blueprint we've been missing. But the truth is, so many of the answers we're chasing are already inside of us.

Sometimes, all we need is stillness to hear them. Sometimes, we just need to *till the soil of our soul*, remove what no longer serves us, and *choose* which seeds we want to continue nurturing. Because growth is not just about what's been planted in you; it's also about what you choose to water.

This chapter is your invitation to pause and ask: "What seeds have been planted in me that I want to grow? And what seeds—planted by fear, trauma, or survival—do I need to uproot?"

You were born with greatness inside of you. But greatness doesn't bloom without intention. It needs awareness. It needs care. It needs room. The garden of your future begins with what you plant, protect, and nurture *right now*.

During one of our most pivotal seasons of self-reflection, Maylin and I discovered the power of returning to simplicity. We realized that in order to grow, heal, and lead with clarity, we needed to *plant the seed of self-care*—not in grand gestures, but in small, intentional routines that honored our minds, bodies, and spirits.

So we began with something sacred: a morning ritual. We made a commitment to start each creative day with a thirty-minute walk—rain or shine. And naturally, the moment we said yes to this practice, the rain came—*every single day that week*. Still, we showed up. On most days, we laced up our shoes and walked through the drizzle, letting the drops fall on our skin like a baptism into the day. And when the rain poured too heavily to venture out, we honored the spirit of our routine by turning inward—choosing meditation, breathwork, or mindful silence instead.

That daily ritual became the soil in which self-care took root.

Planting The Seed

It was a grounding force—carved-out time that was solely ours. No music. No phone calls. No noise. Just the gentle rhythm of our footsteps and the quiet invitation to listen—to our breath, to our thoughts, to the world around us. With every walk, we gave ourselves permission to be fully present. To feel the ground beneath us. To breathe in the morning air. To awaken our senses—sight, sound, smell, touch, and even taste.

In that simplicity, we found clarity. In the rhythm, we found peace. And in those sacred, repetitive moments, we remembered what truly matters: *You can't bloom if you don't first plant and care for the seed.*

Creating a routine—especially one that centers self-care—isn't about perfection. It's about *presence*. It's about showing up for yourself even when conditions aren't ideal. It's about honoring the season you're in while intentionally nurturing the one you're growing into. Because when you consistently water the seed of self-care you don't just feel better—you *become* better. More aligned. More grounded. More whole.

During one of those misty spring mornings, Maylin and I decided to explore an unfamiliar trail near her home. Halfway through, we felt an unexpected sense of enchantment and peace—though it turned out we were trespassing when we spotted a private property sign! Surrounded by the scent of rain-drenched plants and the ancient trees, we listened to the sounds of a rushing creek that was fuller than usual from the rain. It was a magical moment.

As we headed back, I noticed a small budding plant growing amidst the towering, mature trees, reminding me of the photosynthesis lesson I'd learned in my elementary science class. Reflecting on the life cycle of plants, I realized how closely it parallels human growth. Plants need sunlight, air, water, and nutrients from the soil to grow. With these essentials, a seed will sprout, develop roots and leaves, and eventually undergo photosynthesis, converting sunlight into energy for survival.

In many ways, we are like plants. We need to create an intentional environment that supports our growth. We require "sunlight" in the form of positivity and inspiration, "nutrients" in the form of physical and mental nourishment, and "space" to grow, reflect, and breathe. By cultivating these essentials, we can set ourselves up to flourish, just as a little plant grows in a forest of giant trees.

Every transformation begins in the mind. Before you change your habits, your environment, or your relationships, you must first shift your thinking. Because the thoughts you water are the thoughts that grow. And if you're constantly feeding doubt, fear, or limitation, you'll stay rooted in the same place even when your heart is desperate to grow.

Planting the seed of a mindset shift means being willing to challenge your default settings. It's noticing the voice in your head that says, *I'm not ready*, and gently responding with, *But what if I am?* It's choosing to replace the mindset that says, *I always mess things up* with *I'm still learning, and that's okay.*

It begins with an awareness of the beliefs you've inherited, the patterns you've normalized, and the language you speak to yourself every day. Many of these thoughts were planted long ago, through past experiences or survival mode. But just because something *was* doesn't mean it has to *remain*. A mindset shift is not a one-time decision but a daily commitment to reframe, relearn, and rewire. To move from scarcity to abundance. From fear to faith. From passivity to purpose.

When you plant the seed of a new mindset, you begin to see life differently. You start asking different questions. You stop settling for less than what aligns with your worth. You become the gardener of your own growth, choosing what stays, what gets pruned, and what needs to be planted next. And over time, what happens to that seed? It becomes a garden. One that reflects not where you've been but where you're going.

Practice shifting your mindset. If you find yourself stuck in negative thinking, the first step is to start practicing mindfulness. Begin your day by acknowledging what you're grateful for, reframing the narrative from scarcity to abundance.

Let's Practice:

- *Hamster Wheel*: "Here we go again—different day, same stuff."
- **Mindfulness**: "I woke up today! I get another opportunity to experience the world's beauty and wonder."

- *Hamster Wheel*: "Today is going to be so stressful. I have so much to do. What's the point?"
- **Mindfulness**: "Yes, today is busy, but I will still have time to smile, greet others, feel the sunlight, and enjoy the breeze outside."
- *Hamster Wheel*: "I have too many responsibilities. I want to be left alone! I have to pick up the kids, help with homework, cook dinner, and do laundry."
- **Mindfulness**: "I get to pick up my kids, hear about their day, and sit with them for dinner. I get to do laundry at home, listening to my favorite music."

When we approach life with gratitude and intention, we notice how even the smallest tasks add meaning. The mundane transforms as we discover that our routines hold deeper value. Practicing this mindset daily can help us open up to all the good the world offers, which leads to more fulfillment in each day and breaking free from the routine.

We know that shifting your mindset isn't something that happens overnight, and it's easier said than done. But with time and consistent effort, new habits can be formed, helping you move from a hamster-wheel mentality to one rooted in gratitude and growth. Here are some tips to get you started. Remember, this is a journey; take each question and prompt one small step at a time!

SOME SEEDS WE PLANT ON PURPOSE OTHERS ARE PASSED DOWN

Many of the habits we struggle to break, the mindsets that keep us stuck, and the emotional wounds we carry weren't created by us—but they were *inherited*. We were handed beliefs that told us to stay small, silent, or strong even when we were breaking. We were taught to push through pain without processing it, to normalize dysfunction, and to carry burdens that didn't begin with us. But at

Planting The Seed

some point, we must decide: *Do I keep watering what was passed down? Or do I plant something new?*

Breaking cycles—whether behavioral, emotional, or generational—is sacred work. It's not easy though. It requires self-awareness, compassion, and courage. It means questioning the beliefs you were raised with. It means facing the parts of your story that are painful or uncomfortable. It means choosing not to repeat what's been modeled to you simply because it feels familiar.

And here's the truth: You can't heal what you won't name. You can't shift what you're afraid to face. And you can't rise while carrying the weight of everything that tried to break you.

Planting the seed of change starts with one decision: *This stops with me.*

From there, you begin the slow, intentional process of replacing what no longer serves you with what supports who you are becoming. You begin to rewrite the script. You choose self-awareness over blame. Healing over hiding. Growth over generational pain.

Every small act—whether it's going to therapy, journaling, setting boundaries, or learning how to rest—is a seed planted in new soil. You're not just transforming yourself; you're changing the landscape for those who come after you.

And that? That is legacy work.

A seed doesn't bloom overnight.

It doesn't even look like anything is happening for a while. But underneath the surface? Transformation is taking place.

And so it is with us.

Your daily efforts matter. Your small wins matter. The way you speak to yourself *matters*. Even one intentional moment each day has the power to redirect your entire life over time.

Instead of being overwhelmed by how far you have to go, focus on how far you've come. And then focus on your next step. One new thought. One healthy boundary. One tiny act of courage. That's how new roots are formed.

You are not just healing for yourself in this moment. You are healing for your future. You are building a life your younger self dreamed of and your future self will thank you for. This is the season of sowing, so don't be discouraged when you don't see the full harvest yet. Tend to your soil. Water your progress. Keep showing up.

Every day is an opportunity to grow, to push a little farther, to make one decision that reflects who you're becoming—not who you used to be. The seed has already been planted by your desire to change.

Now it's time to nurture it—with love, discipline, grace, and vision.

Growing up, seeds were planted in me through words of encouragement, knowing glances, and moments when someone saw something in me I couldn't yet see in myself. I didn't have the language for it then, but I now recognize how deeply those early acts of belief shaped me. I was fortunate to be surrounded by women—peers and elders—who modeled what it looked like to support one another without competition. Back then, we just called it love and friendship; today, I know it as sisterhood and the beginning of a lifelong calling to uplift others the same way I was uplifted.

The mentors in my life—though I didn't know to call them that at the time—taught me through presence, consistency, and compassion. Their guidance was the quiet voice reminding me to choose wisely even when no one was watching. Those seeds of mentorship, support, and sisterhood became the roots of the woman I am today. Through years of hard work, both in faith and in failure, I now understand that the foundation they helped cultivate was preparing me to become the guide, the sister, and the mentor for others. And so I plant forward—intentionally, lovingly, faithfully—trusting that every seed sown today becomes part of someone else's garden tomorrow.

CULTIVATING FRUITFUL HABITS

Once a seed is planted, it doesn't grow overnight. It requires nurturing—consistent care, the right environment, and a daily commitment to its development. The same is true for the habits that shape our lives.

Habits are the water, sunlight, and structure that support the seeds we've planted. Without them, our intentions can wither. But when we intentionally choose habits that align with our values and vision, we begin to cultivate a life that is not only stable but deeply fulfilling.

Creating fruitful habits isn't about perfection; it's about *purpose*. These habits are formed in the daily decision to honor your growth, one action at a time. The habits you build are like the water and sunlight for the seeds you've planted; they help your intentions take root and thrive.

Developing habits that truly enrich your life takes intentionality, patience, and a clear plan. Don't rush the process by trying to do everything at once. It doesn't work that way. Instead, you must consistently choose what aligns with who you are becoming.

Here are some simple steps to help you begin cultivating habits that will support your growth and help you thrive:

Step 1: Define Your Desired Habit.

Be specific about the habit you want to cultivate. Instead of vague goals, make them SMART: Specific, Measurable, Achievable, Relevant, and Time-bound. For example, rather than saying, "I want to exercise more," reframe it: "I will jog for thirty minutes every morning before work." Clarity helps turn aspirations into actionable steps.

Step 2: Start Small and Build Consistency.
Break your habit into smaller, manageable steps. Begin with a commitment you can easily incorporate into your daily routine. For example, start by jogging for five to ten minutes instead of thirty, which can feel overwhelming at first. As you build consistency and confidence, gradually increase the duration or intensity. Remember, success lies in creating a regular pattern of behavior rather than bombarding yourself with unrealistic goals.

Step 3: Make It Easy.
Prepare everything you need the night before so it's simple to follow through. Lay out your clothes, socks, and shoes where you'll see them first thing in the morning. The fewer steps you have to take, the better. Our minds tend to resist anything that feels like effort, so make it as effortless as possible to stick to your new habit.

Step 4: Use Positive Reinforcement and Accountability.
Celebrate your progress no matter how small. Positive reinforcement can keep you motivated and excited about your journey. Treat yourself to something meaningful when you hit milestones—whether it's a new book, a favorite meal, or simply taking a moment to acknowledge your growth. Additionally, enlist an accountability partner, or leverage tools like habit-tracking apps to stay consistent. Sharing your goals with someone you trust can provide extra encouragement and support.

Step 5: Embrace Patience and Persistence.
Building fruitful habits is a gradual process. Expect occasional setbacks and view them as opportunities to learn and adjust. Stay

Planting The Seed

focused on your long-term goals, and be kind to yourself along the way. Over time, these habits will not only become second nature but will also create lasting positive changes in your life. With intentionality and persistence, your fruitful habits will bloom into a more fulfilled and purposeful life.

Change doesn't happen all at once. It happens in moments. In decisions. In whispers. In the stillness of the morning when you decide to speak an affirmation instead of absorbing anxiety. In the quiet pause between a triggered thought and a new response. That is where the seed is planted.

💧 Christina
🦋 Maylin

PAUSE, REFLECT, AND REACT

Planting the Seed with Intention

This exercise is designed to help you slow down and examine the internal seeds you've inherited, absorbed, or unintentionally nurtured and then begin intentionally planting the ones that align with your growth.

PAUSE

Take a few deep breaths. Get still. Clear some space both physically and mentally. Ask yourself:

- What patterns or beliefs have I been repeating without question?
- Am I acting from a place of truth or survival?
- What emotions have I been pushing aside that need my attention?

Tip: Sometimes a pause looks like silence, a walk, or just closing your eyes and placing your hand on your heart. Honor whatever stillness looks like for you.

REFLECT

Use these prompts to dig deeper into what has been planted and what needs to be uprooted or nurtured:

1. What habits or mindsets were planted during my childhood or past experiences that I still carry today (fear of failure, people-pleasing, emotional suppression, perfectionism)?
2. Which of these have helped me grow? Which have held me back?

3. What generational patterns or traumas do I want to stop passing down—whether to my children, my community, or my inner self?
4. What new mindset, boundary, or habit do I want to intentionally plant and grow moving forward?

REACT

Now that you've paused and reflected, it's time to take intentional action: planting a new seed that will support your next chapter.

Choose *one* small but meaningful step you can take this week:

- Start a five-minute morning routine to shift your mindset.
- Write a forgiveness letter to release past hurt.
- Set a new boundary and stick to it, even if it feels uncomfortable.
- Say one kind thing to yourself each day out loud.

WRITE IT DOWN

This week, I will plant the seed of _____ by _____.

Remember: You don't need to change your whole life in one day. You just need to *plant the seed.* Water it. Protect it. And trust that growth will come.

CHAPTER 4

Can Your No Mean No?

Say no to the good so you can say yes to the great.
—JOHN MAXWELL

CREATING HEALTHY BOUNDARIES and learning to say no are essential skills for achieving personal and professional success. The reality is, you can't be all things to all people, and it's time you begin to normalize the power and freedom in saying no to things that don't align with your priorities. Setting boundaries doesn't make you a bad person; it makes you aware of your capacity and positions you to live more intentionally.

Over the years, we've had firsthand experience and witnessed the impact of moving outside of our capacity. I can assure you going any extended period in that direction will not only negatively impact your physical and mental health, but could also impact relationships that are meaningful (spouse, children, close friends) and hinder your business revenue. Establishing boundaries encourages mutual respect in relationships in personal and professional settings.

For as long as I can remember, accepting changes in relationships—especially when separation was involved—was incredibly hard for me. Whether it was a friendship, a professional connection, or a working environment, I often internalized the ending as a personal failure. I'd question if I was being a bad friend, a disloyal employee, or somehow not grateful enough. Even when I *knew* deep down that the relationship had run its course or was hindering my growth, I struggled with the guilt of letting go.

It wasn't until well into my professional career that I began to understand a simple but profound truth: The way people treat you is based on what *you* allow and teach them. Once I started standing firm in my boundaries and saying no without over-explaining or apologizing, the dynamics around me began to shift. Some relationships faded naturally, and while it was painful at first, it created space for personal growth and deep self-reflection.

Getting to that place, however, took time. Some people are naturally assertive and have no problem vocalizing their needs, expectations, or boundaries. That wasn't my story. Earlier in my career, when I said yes to something I *knew* I should've declined, I would replay the entire conversation in my head for days. I'd analyze every word, trying to figure out what I could have said differently to avoid overcommitting or disappointing someone.

So I began to practice saying no—out loud, in the mirror, and eventually, in real-time situations. The more confident I became in who I was and the value I brought to the table, the less I felt the need to be accepted. It became less about people-pleasing and more about *harnessing* my contributions with intention.

Over time, I also learned the power of my *voice* and my *silence*.

People often comment that I'm quiet and reserved until something calls for me to speak. When that moment comes, I speak with clarity, conviction, and purpose. It often catches people off guard—in a good way. They'll say, "Wow, I didn't know you had that in you." But what they don't realize is that I've trained myself to listen first, deeply and intentionally. I don't speak just to speak. I speak when it matters.

That quiet space between impulse and action is where my power lives. It's in that stillness that I remember who I am and what I stand for. I no longer feel the need to over-explain or react out of emotion—because grounded in discernment, I trust myself. And sometimes the most powerful move isn't saying more—it's choosing peace and protecting your alignment at all costs.

THE POWER OF SAYING NO

Learning to say no is one of the most empowering tools in personal and professional development. For many of us, especially those who value being dependable or helpful, saying no can feel uncomfortable, like we're letting others down. But the truth is, setting boundaries is a form of self-respect. It creates space for alignment, rest, and real growth.

To confidently say no, you have to know your personal boundaries, nonnegotiables, and priority areas. If you haven't taken time to reflect on who you are and how you want to show up, others will do the defining for you.

Here are a few practical strategies to help you set boundaries and respond with confidence:

- *Be clear and direct*: Politely decline using simple language like, "I'm sorry, I can't take this on right now."
- *Offer alternatives*: If appropriate, suggest another solution or resource.

- *Practice self-awareness*: Know your emotional and time limitations to avoid burnout.
- *Stay firm*: Others may try to change your mind, but stand in your decision.
- *Be honest without over-explaining*: A short, genuine reason is enough.

BUILDING HEALTHY BOUNDARIES AT WORK

Work culture is changing, and it's important to know what matters most to *you* in a professional environment. While salary is important, consider other values that impact your well-being:

Ask yourself:

- Does this company allow for flexibility or remote work?
- Are there leadership or professional-development opportunities?
- Do they support mental and physical wellness?
- Is communication encouraged and respected?

Companies that align with your values can create a life-enhancing work experience. Use these strategies to support healthy boundaries at work:

- *Define work hours*: Communicate clear start and end times to avoid overextension.
- *Delegate wisely*: Avoid burnout by sharing tasks when appropriate.
- *Set clear expectations*: Know what's expected of you and advocate when things shift.
- *Take breaks*: Build rest into your day to maintain focus and energy.
- *Seek support*: Utilize HR, a mentor, or an ally if boundaries are being crossed.

BOUNDARIES IN YOUR PERSONAL LIFE

Boundaries at home and in relationships are just as vital. These help preserve your energy, protect your peace, and support healthy connections.

- *Communicate your needs*: Be open about your emotional and time boundaries.
- *Limit accessibility*: Protect your downtime. Don't feel obligated to be available 24/7.
- *Prioritize what matters*: Choose commitments that align with your values.
- *Respect others' boundaries*: Lead by example in honoring others' limits.
- *Practice regular self-reflection*: Check in with yourself and adjust as needed.

Implementing boundaries doesn't always come easy, especially if you're used to saying yes out of guilt or habit. But with practice, it gets easier. Learn to manage your guilt. Saying no is not a rejection of another; it's self-care. You will also need to learn how to handle pushback by standing firm in your truth even when others resist.

We know, this might feel like a lot. But here's your reminder: This process doesn't require you doing everything at once. It's about taking things one day, one moment, one intentional step at a time. Start small. Start where you are. Then gently integrate these strategies into your daily life.

The real starting point is *awareness*. Once you're aware of what needs to shift, that awareness becomes the seed for change. From there, it's about taking aligned action—bit by bit, breath by breath.

There comes a time in every journey when you must confront the uncomfortable truth that *you are not obligated to carry everything*. You are not required to attend every event, say yes to every favor, or accept every opportunity, especially when these things pull you away from what matters most.

For far too long, many of us have worn the title of "dependable," "the strong one," or "always available" like a badge of honor, without realizing the weight it places on our well-being, focus, and purpose. We were never taught that *no* is not a rejection. So we must now see it is a redirection. Saying no is an act of self-respect. It's a declaration that your time, your energy, and your peace are *sacred*. Declining someone's request doesn't mean you're selfish. It means you're intentional. It means you're choosing alignment over approval, purpose over pressure, peace over pleasing.

Every time you say yes to something that doesn't align with your goals, you're potentially saying no to something that does. Your bandwidth isn't infinite. Your calendar isn't elastic. Your energy is not renewable if you never pause to recharge.

Boundaries are not walls to keep others out. They're bridges that help *you* stay in alignment with *you*. They help you filter the noise, eliminate distractions, and stay grounded in what you're building. When you say no with confidence and clarity, you create space for saying yes to the important things—yes to growth, yes to purpose, yes to rest, yes to the version of you that is rising.

The advice in this chapter is your permission slip to:

- Say no to overcommitting out of guilt.
- Say no to relationships that drain you.
- Say no to requests that feel more like demands.
- Say no to the hustle that leads to burnout.

You get to set the tone. You get to define your limits. You get to reframe the belief that saying no is rude, selfish, or unkind. In reality, a clear no is often more respectful than a reluctant yes.

When your no becomes honest, your yes becomes powerful.

Can Your No Mean No?

For so long, I said yes to everything. Not because I had the time or energy, but because I didn't want to disappoint anyone. I thought my no would hurt people, appear selfish, or make me less lovable. I got so used to showing up for everyone else that I ignored my own needs. I remember one day scrolling through Facebook and realizing I had literally attended ten different events in one day. Ten. That moment shocked me. I couldn't believe how much I was running on empty just to keep up with an identity I thought I had to uphold. As time passed and my responsibilities grew, the impact started to show—in my health, my peace, and my ability to be fully present.

I slowly started making changes. I began RSVPing "maybe" or "interested" instead of automatically saying yes. If I truly couldn't attend, I'd still support by donating, gifting products, or sending love from afar. That shift gave me the necessary space to rest, to heal, and to face parts of myself I had long avoided. I had to confront the story I'd been telling myself: In order to be loved, I had to be everything to everyone. Letting go of that belief was hard, but replacing it with truth was freeing. Now I remind myself: Those who truly love me will understand when I show up from a place of joy, not guilt. Saying yes with intention has made my life richer, more peaceful, and far more aligned with the woman I'm becoming.

Start small if you have to. One clear, intentional no can open the door to a hundred aligned yeses. Saying no doesn't make you difficult. It doesn't make you selfish. It makes you aware of your capacity, your values, and your vision for who you are becoming.

You weren't placed on this earth to be everything to everyone. You are here to be everything to you: to honor the healed, grounded, and focused version of yourself that's waiting to bloom. And that requires protecting your energy, nurturing your growth, and planting seeds that reflect where you want to go, not just where you've been.

THE JOURNEY

Your no is not just a word. It's a boundary. It's a decision. It's a declaration. Every time you say no to what drains you, you are saying yes to what feeds you. To rest. To peace. To purpose. To alignment. And the more you practice choosing from that place of intention, the more your life begins to reflect the very seeds you've planted.

You don't need to do it all today. But you do need to begin. Because every beautiful harvest begins with one brave seed—and a commitment to tend to it, day by day.

◆ Christina
🦋 Maylin

PAUSE, REFLECT, AND REACT

Releasing to Rise

Take a moment to sit with the stillness. Let these questions guide you as you evaluate the spaces, people, and patterns in your life that may be overdue for a shift.

1. What conversation or relationship have I been holding onto that no longer serves me? Why am I holding on? What am I afraid to release?
2. Where in my life am I saying yes out of guilt, obligation, or fear of disappointing others? How is that affecting my energy, peace, and growth?
3. How have I been teaching others to treat me through what I tolerate or avoid addressing? What new boundary or expectation do I need to communicate moving forward?
4. When was the last time I listened to my intuition but ignored it? What did that moment teach me about trusting myself?
5. What does it look like to honor my voice and my silence equally? How can I use both to navigate relationships with clarity and confidence?

CHAPTER 5

The Power of Proximity

You don't just grow because of what's within you. You grow because of who's around you.
—CHRISTINA VERA

THERE'S A SAYING that says, "If you want to go fast, go alone. If you want to go far, go together." But the truth is, *who* you go with matters just as much as where you're going. Every step of your journey—whether personal, spiritual, or professional—is influenced by the people walking beside you. The conversations you're having, the values being modeled around you, the energy being exchanged—all of it plays a role in shaping your mindset, your motivation, and your momentum. This is the power of proximity. The people closest to you don't just reflect your present, they also influence your future.

The people you surround yourself with can either water your growth or stunt your progress. In this chapter, we'll explore the powerful impact that our relationships and social circles have on both our personal and professional development. From mindset to motivation, the energy we expose ourselves to plays a critical role in shaping our confidence, our decisions, and the direction of our lives. By reflecting on these dynamics, we gain clarity on which relationships are aligned with our purpose and which ones may be silently holding us back. This awareness empowers us to choose connection over convenience and alignment over attachment.

ENERGY IS CONTAGIOUS

Whether we're conscious of it or not, we are always absorbing energy. It's in the conversations we engage in, the rooms we enter, the social media posts we scroll past, and most deeply, in the people we engage with. There is a constant, invisible exchange happening—one that doesn't always speak but is always felt.

This transfer of energy has the power to either elevate or exhaust us. The people closest to you are shaping your mindset in real time. Are you surrounded by dreamers who challenge you to rise, or doubters who subtly plant seeds of hesitation? Are you in the company of builders who speak life into your vision, or breakers who silently compete while pretending to support you?

This isn't about placing blame or labeling others; it's about *awareness*. Because without awareness, we carry invisible weight from relationships that chip away at our confidence and tether us to a version of ourselves we have outgrown.

Negative energy doesn't always arrive with a red flag. Sometimes it hides in passive-aggressive comments masked as jokes, or in the silence that follows your wins. It can come from friends, coworkers, even family—people who may mean well but, driven by fear or unhealed wounds, project their limitations onto your dreams. Over time, this energy dims your light. You start doubting your voice, hesitating before taking up space, and managing other people's comfort instead of pursuing your own calling.

The Power of Proximity

But just as energy can drag you down, it can also lift you. Being in proximity to people who are aligned—who lead with intention, walk in integrity, and believe in your becoming—can expand your vision in ways you never imagined. These are the people who don't compete with your growth; they *contribute* to it. Their energy affirms your purpose, celebrates your progress, and reminds you that you are not too much. You are more than enough.

Your body always knows. Long before your mind tries to rationalize someone's behavior, your energy will shift. Pay attention to how you feel after spending time with someone: Do you feel lighter or heavier? Seen or dismissed? Grounded or anxious? These cues are emotional as well as spiritual. They are also the early warning signs of what needs to be protected or released.

You may not be able to control every space you enter, but you *can* control what you carry with you. That's where energetic boundaries come in. You have the right to decide what and who is allowed to shape your day, your spirit, and your story. That might mean limiting time with certain people, adding space to your schedule for recovery, or intentionally seeking out environments that inspire growth, not survival.

You don't have to be rude to protect your peace. You just have to be clear. Your energy is sacred—and so is your journey. Your circle doesn't need to be big. But it does need to be *aligned*. Because your dreams are too valuable to be surrounded by people who aren't equipped to honor them. Surround yourself with those who charge your spirit, not those who quietly deplete it.

Your energy serves as your compass. Protect it fiercely.

Growing up, I always felt a strong sense of responsibility for others. I think part of that came from being the oldest of four siblings and watching my mother navigate life and parenthood on her own for much of my childhood. Most of my elementary and middle school years were shaped by survival, not stability. There wasn't much support, and the emotional weight of that fell heavily on me. I witnessed a lot of toxicity in my early environment. I can say all this now, without judgment, because in hindsight, I truly believe that the adults around me were doing the best they could, given the tools and exposure they had available.

As I transitioned into my teenage years, chaos began to feel like home. I gravitated toward people and environments that mirrored the internal unrest I hadn't yet learned to name. I found myself running with crowds that had little regard for others—and sometimes, even less regard for life. But that didn't scare me. It felt familiar. Through therapy and deep reflection, I would later come to understand that my comfort with dysfunction was rooted in an abandonment complex shaped by my relationship with my father. For years, I equated loyalty with endurance, to my own detriment. Leaving unhealthy relationships or jobs felt like betrayal, not self-preservation.

As I reflected on the influence of the people around me, I connected with Michelle Ferrigno Warren's book, *The Power of Proximity*, and realized just how much of my stagnation was tied not only to my decisions, but to the people I allowed into my life.[1] Some were comfortable with the unhealed version of me because she didn't challenge them. She stayed small to keep the peace. But peace isn't the absence of conflict; it's the presence of clarity.

Things began to shift when I met Maylin over sixteen years ago. At the time, I had no history with her, so she owed me nothing. And yet, she gave me everything. She showed up with kindness, encouragement, and unwavering support. I always believed I was loyal, but watching Maylin come through for me in ways I had never experienced helped me redefine what *reciprocal* loyalty actually looks like. Her love didn't require trauma to prove itself. Once I experienced that kind of safety and sisterhood, it changed me. I could no longer settle for conditional love, convenient friendships, or relationships that fed off of my silence.

That clarity gave me the strength to start letting go—of friendships built on convenience, family ties bound by generational trauma, and romantic relationships rooted in betrayal, manipulation, or emotional neglect. Maylin exposed me to what was possible, and, more importantly, what I *deserved*.

At the beginning of this transformation, I was a mother of two. Now I'm a mother of three. But even then, I knew they were watching. Watching how I treated others. Watching how I allowed others to treat me. Watching how I navigated hard conversations, heartbreak, and healing. And I had to ask myself, *What environment am I modeling for my children?* What legacy am I passing down—not just through my words, but through the energy and boundaries I create?

I had to shift my mindset from survival mode to intentional living. I had to decide that just getting through the day wasn't enough. I wanted to *build* a life that reflected the healing, peace, and purpose I was chasing. And that meant stripping away what no longer aligned with my values and vision. That meant choosing myself. It wasn't easy. But it was necessary.

Looking back, I know with every fiber of my being that I wouldn't be the woman I am today had I not taken an honest inventory of my life and relationships and then made the *choice*—followed by action—to move differently.

What I know to be true now is this: Loyalty should be earned, not freely given. Loyalty is a powerful and beautiful quality, but it should never be blind or one-sided. True devotion must be mutual. It should be rooted in consistent action, respect, and care—not history or obligation.

It took years—and more than a few missed opportunities—for me to learn that I had been misplacing my loyalty, time, and energy. But letting go of drama-filled relationships and emotionally draining friendships created a peace I can only describe as sacred. At this stage in my life, if I call you a friend or invite you into my space, know that I have taken the time to reflect, pray, and evaluate whether the relationship is life-giving. Because I now understand that *healthy relationships don't drain you; they sustain you.* And when we learn that loyalty must be *earned*, we set the foundation for deeper trust, stronger boundaries, and relationships that are built to last.

THE POSITIVE INFLUENCE OF HEALTHY RELATIONSHIPS

Comfort can be costly. Many of us stay connected to people out of history, not alignment. We confuse loyalty with obligation and shrink ourselves to maintain familiar dynamics. But growth often requires uncomfortable choices—like outgrowing friendships or distancing from relationships that no longer serve who we're becoming. That isn't a lack of love for others; it's a deepening love and respect for yourself.

Healthy relationships are supportive *and* transformative. The right people don't just cheer you on, they also challenge you, hold you accountable, and reflect your potential back to you, even when you can't see it yourself. When rooted in mutual respect, trust, and shared values, these relationships become a powerful foundation for both personal and professional success.

Take a moment to audit your circle. Who inspires you? Who drains you? Who truly wants to see you win? And who only shows up when it benefits them? Not everyone is meant to go where you're going, and that's okay. Letting go doesn't always mean conflict; sometimes it just means moving forward with clarity and peace.

Following are some key ways healthy relationships can fuel your growth:

- *Support & Encouragement:* The right people believe in you, offer emotional support, and motivate you to keep going.
- *Constructive Feedback*: Trusted voices can offer honest, loving feedback that pushes you to improve.
- *Network & Opportunities*: Strong, aligned connections can open doors to jobs, partnerships, and new ventures.
- *Accountability*: Goal-driven relationships help you stay focused, committed, and on track.

Surround yourself with people who light your fire, not those who dim your spark.

HOW RELATIONSHIPS CAN HINDER GROWTH

Every person in your circle is either helping you climb or quietly making the climb harder. The higher you rise in life, the more intentional you must be about the energy surrounding you. Not everyone will understand your growth, your boundaries, or your evolving sense of purpose. The truth is, not everyone needs to. Your responsibility is to protect your vision and preserve your path. Because climbing with the wrong people is how you fall. Climbing with the right people? That's how you rise. Our environment—especially the people closest to us—plays a powerful role in shaping our thoughts, behaviors, and outcomes. When we allow unhealthy relationships to linger unchecked, they can subtly but steadily derail our growth, drain our ambition, and distort our sense of self. Being selective about your circle isn't selfish; it's strategic.

Not all relationships are rooted in support. If left unchecked, some can quietly derail your progress. The people you surround yourself with influence your mindset, energy, and ambition. Be aware of how certain relationships can hinder your growth:

- **Negative Mindset:** Constant exposure to pessimism, criticism, or limiting beliefs can wear down your

confidence. When you're surrounded by people who focus on what's wrong or what's impossible, it becomes harder to believe in your own potential or take bold steps forward.
- **Distractions and Drains:** Some relationships demand your energy without giving anything in return. These emotional or mental drains can leave you depleted, distracted, and disconnected from your goals. You can't pour into your purpose when you're constantly being emptied by others.
- **Stagnation:** Being in the company of individuals who lack vision or discourage growth can lead to complacency. If the people around you are comfortable staying the same, you may begin to shrink your own goals just to fit in. Growth thrives in challenge, and stagnation often stems from a circle that doesn't challenge you to evolve.
- **Toxic Influence:** Manipulative, controlling, or abusive relationships can do lasting damage to your mental health, self-worth, and overall well-being. These dynamics not only affect your emotional balance, but they also pull focus and energy away from your progress, keeping you in survival mode instead of growth mode.

Being mindful of who has access to your energy is not about judgment; it's about alignment. Healthy relationships elevate you; unhealthy ones limit you. The choice to protect your peace is also a choice to protect your potential.

The company we keep profoundly impacts our journey toward personal and professional success. By surrounding ourselves with positive, supportive, and growth-oriented individuals, we can enhance our chances of achieving our goals. Conversely, recognizing and addressing the influence of negative relationships is essential for protecting our well-being and progress. In the pursuit of success, it is crucial to cultivate a social circle that aligns with and supports our aspirations. It's not just about who's around you—it's about who's *pouring into* you. The right circle will challenge you, celebrate you, and remind you of your worth when you forget. They'll speak life into your vision and hold you accountable to the version of yourself you're becoming, not just the one you've been. On the flip side, staying connected to people who drain your energy, diminish your dreams, or thrive in chaos can silently sabotage your growth. Sometimes, choosing success means having the courage to create distance, set boundaries, or walk away from relationships that no longer serve your evolution. You don't owe anyone access to a version of you they refuse to grow with. Protect your space—it's sacred. Because the environment you build around you will either elevate or exhaust you.

CHOOSE YOUR PARTNER WISELY

The most important thing we can tell you about marriage is this: Don't just choose love. Choose alignment. Love focuses on feelings while alignment focuses on a shared understanding, purpose, and perspective. Choosing your partner wisely is one of the most important decisions you'll ever make. It's the foundation of your emotional, spiritual, and mental well-being. Never forget—it's better to be single than to settle for something that misaligns with your values or diminishes your worth. Being single doesn't mean being alone. Being single means you are strong enough to wait for love that honors your healing, reflects your wholeness, and supports your purpose. You are worthy of a love that meets you where you are and grows with you toward where you're going.

Choosing your life partner is one of the most important decisions you will ever make. I wish someone had told me this when I was younger. Unlike some girls who dream of weddings and fairytales, I didn't picture myself getting married. In fact, I wasn't dreaming of love at all. I was dreaming of running away. Growing up, my home was filled with chaos, betrayal, and pain. The glimpses of love I saw were not enough to model how to be healthy. I don't blame my parents; they could only show me what they knew as they, too, were on their own journey. But witnessing the turmoil at home made me long for something different. Disney movies became my escape, and I fantasized about their joyful stories and happy endings. As my family fell apart, I couldn't shake the feeling that it was somehow my fault. I thought I should have been able to save my parents' relationship and keep us together.

And yet, even in the midst of that chaos, I experienced resilience. I experienced a form of love that didn't always know how to be soft or healthy—love that was tangled in survival, tradition, and unhealed wounds. There were moments of care, but they were often buried beneath cultural norms that equated masculinity with control rather than compassion. Society praised the macho mentality, but it rarely made space for emotional intelligence or therapy. I often felt loved and unloved at the same time; held and hurt by the same hands. Looking back, I realize that what I was craving wasn't perfection; it was emotional safety, representation, and the tools for healing that we simply didn't have access to at the time. Still, through it all—through my faith, therapy, meditation, energy work, and the presence of a few soul-aligned people who modeled healthy love and friendship—I discovered resilience, reclaimed my worth, and found the courage to break generational cycles.

That sense of failure shaped me deeply. I developed people-pleasing tendencies and carried an overwhelming fear of abandonment like a shadow. Therapy wasn't even on my radar because I didn't know it was an option. So I threw myself into what I could control: school. I promised myself I'd never depend on a man to survive. My mother's voice echoed in my mind like a

The Power of Proximity

sacred truth: Un hombre puede dejarte, puedes perder tu trabajo, pero tu educación, mi hija—eso es tuyo. Nadie te lo puede quitar. (A man can leave you, you can lose your job, but your education, my daughter—that is yours. No one can take it away from you.) That became my fuel. I poured my heart into my studies, determined to build a life no one could strip away. But life had other plans, and some of its most powerful lessons came dressed as love.

There were a few people who became my greatest teachers, though they taught me through pain, not peace. These were the partners I invited into my world, trusting their promises of loyalty, protection, and love. At first, I stayed guarded—wary, cautious, self-protective. But over time, they learned my fears, my longing for love (not necessarily a fairytale, just something safe and true), and the quiet ache from wounds I hadn't yet healed. They told me I was safe. That they'd never lie or betray me. That I was worthy of real joy and lasting love. And I wanted so badly to believe them, so I did. I even said yes to a ring, hoping maybe this was the happy ending I had once dreamed of. But it wasn't.

If you're nodding along or wondering how someone wise and accomplished could fall for this, let me explain: Sometimes we attract what we are trying to heal. You may meet someone and sense that they are not right for you, but you tell yourself it's just a professional or friendly connection. There's nothing to worry about. Then they show you the version of themselves that they know you deserve—the charming, caring, and attentive version. You start to believe that maybe they really are different, better, and worthy of your trust. You ignore your intuition, choosing to focus on how good it feels to be seen and loved. It's easy to ignore red flags when someone is giving you what your soul has longed for.

But I own my choices and the consequences they brought. Those relationships were part of my journey, shaping the woman I am today who is wiser, stronger, and more aligned with my true self. I now understand that every encounter is a lesson, and not everyone deserves access to my heart. Most importantly, I've become the partner I want to attract: secure, intuitive, and filled with self-love. Through it all, I've learned that choosing your partner wisely means choosing yourself first, knowing your worth and never settling for less than you deserve.

A person who presents a curated or false version of themselves is what we refer to as an Imposter Representative: someone who selectively showcases traits or behaviors to gain trust, acceptance, or influence while concealing their true intentions or identity. Over time, their actions often reveal that they are the opposite of who they initially portrayed themselves to be.

Let's explore how you can recognize and filter out the Imposter Representative (IR) when navigating relationships.

1. **Identify Your Nonnegotiables.** Before entering a relationship, make a list of your core values and dealbreakers—those attributes and behaviors you absolutely need in a partner, like honesty, respect, spiritual beliefs, and shared goals. Observe whether their actions consistently align with these values. Words can be deceiving, but consistent actions reveal true character.
2. **Assess Their Integrity and Honesty.** Pay close attention to the consistency of their stories over time. Do they change details or make excuses frequently? Genuine partners are transparent about their past, present, and future intentions. Be wary of those who evade questions or act secretive about significant aspects of their life. Notice if they lie about who they are to others or present a false version of themselves.
3. **Observe Their Treatment of Others.** A person's character is often revealed by how they treat those around them, including waitstaff, family, and friends. Consistent kindness and respect toward others are good

indicators of their true nature. While you don't need to dig too deep into their past, pay attention to how they speak about previous relationships. Are they respectful or quick to place all the blame on the other person?

4. **Evaluate Emotional and Mental Health.** Emotional stability is key in any healthy relationship. Notice how your partner handles stress, conflict, or loss. Do they remain respectful or resort to manipulation? A supportive partner will encourage your personal growth and uplift you. If they don't believe in your dreams or show consistent support, then it's time to reevaluate.

5. **Look for Shared Goals and Values.** Long-term compatibility thrives on shared values and future aspirations. Have open conversations about your goals—whether it's career paths, having children, or lifestyle choices. Make sure your core beliefs about family, spiritual, finances, and other significant aspects of life are aligned.

6. **Be Patient. Time Will Tell.** Give the relationship time to evolve. A year (four seasons) is a good time period to truly experience your partner and observe patterns in their behavior. Consistency over time is more telling than a few charming gestures.

7. **Trust Your Intuition, and Seek External Insights.** Listen to your gut. If something feels off, don't ignore it. Your intuition can pick up on red flags that your mind might rationalize away. Also, seek the perspectives of close friends and family. They might see what you can't.

Now let's talk about the flip side of the discovery phase: the part we don't always want to admit. You can go through this journey of self-awareness with metaphorical sunglasses on, never daring to take a real look in the mirror. It's easy to point out flaws in other people: what they're doing wrong, how they're showing up, what they're lacking. But how often do we pause to evaluate ourselves? How often do we ask, "Am I actually the one pretending? Am I the Imposter Representative in this situation?"

You know what I mean. When we first meet someone—whether in business, friendships, or romantic relationships—we tend to put on a show. We highlight the best parts of ourselves, sometimes to the point of performance. We go above and beyond—our appearance, the experiences we curate, the gifts we give, even the meals we cook (if that's your thing; personally, that's never been my ministry, but you get the point). We try so hard to impress.

But what happens six months to a year down the line when the mask slips? When the effort fades and the performance softens? Suddenly, things feel "off," but is it really the other person, or is it the shift in our own consistency?

Here's the truth: You can't manifest a partner, friend group, or career that you're not actually willing or ready to rise up and match. "You get what you give" holds weight—*sometimes*. But let's be real. It doesn't always work that way. That's why self-evaluation is so necessary. If you're giving authentically, pouring into others, and receiving nothing in return, it may be time to accept that you're trying to grow in the wrong garden. No amount of energy, time, or prayer can make someone ready for what you're offering if it's not aligned.

On the flip side, if you *do* have people in your life who are pouring into your social and emotional battery, who show up for you consistently, it's worth asking: "What am I bringing to the table?" Or better yet: "Am I the table?" Are you contributing love, support, growth, truth, and effort the way you want it reciprocated?

I'll give you a personal example. When my husband and I first met, I was only sixteen years old. The man I met back then and the man he is now (twenty-four years later) are not the same. Just like I am no longer that teenage girl he met. We've both evolved and faced some hard seasons and growth opportunities—together and apart. We've even had periods where we had to take time and space to figure out who we were as individuals.

One of the most profound things I had to learn was this: My husband is not solely responsible for my happiness or fulfillment. Sure, he contributes to it, and I'm grateful for that. But it's not his job to convince me that I am loved simply by existing. That's *my job*. It's my responsibility to know that I'm enough, that I am worthy of love, and that I bring value to the relationship. And when I have that to give, I also have the responsibility to reciprocate it.

Before you point fingers or assign blame, ask yourself: *"Am I being the kind of person I want to attract? Am I showing up with honesty, integrity, and effort? Or am I expecting others to fill shoes I haven't even stepped into myself?"* It's easy to focus on what others are lacking, but real growth begins when you turn inward and take responsibility for the energy you bring into every space. You can't demand loyalty if you're inconsistent. You can't expect deep connections if you only show up on the surface. And you can't ask others to support your dreams when you haven't fully committed to them yourself. When you elevate your own standards—how you speak, how you give, how you lead—you naturally begin to attract people who reflect that same frequency. Alignment starts with you. Be who you say you are, and you'll find that the right people will meet you there.

GUARD THE GATE TO YOUR GROWTH

The truth is, you're not just building a life—you're climbing toward purpose. And every person you allow into your space either adds weight to your climb or gives you the wind to rise. Your circle has power. It shapes how you think, how you feel, how you dream, and how far you're willing to go.

THE JOURNEY

Growth requires both strategy and *discernment*. And discernment begins with understanding that not everyone who claps is for you. Not everyone who shows up is meant to stay. And not everyone who walks with you is prepared to climb with you. Surround yourself with people who mirror your values, amplify your vision, and honor your boundaries. Choose those who challenge you without competing, hold you accountable without controlling, and love you without conditions. These are the ones who deserve access to your most sacred spaces.

Your proximity is your power. Guard it with intention. Your climb is too important—and your purpose too sacred—to carry the weight of relationships that were never meant to go the distance.

♦ Christina
🦋 Maylin

PAUSE, REFLECT, AND REACT

Relationships as Reflections

As you move forward on your journey of self-awareness and growth, take time to pause and evaluate the relationships in your life with intention. Whether romantic, platonic, or professional, your connections should reflect the life you're building and not pull you back into a version of yourself you've outgrown.

A truly compatible partner—whether in love or life—will respect your values, walk in integrity, and align with your vision for the future. Reflect on the following prompts to gain clarity, set boundaries, and build a foundation rooted in truth and alignment.

1. List Your Nonnegotiables
    » Identify your core values and deal-breakers.
    » What principles guide your life?
    » What are the boundaries you refuse to compromise on in a relationship?
2. Analyze Current or Past Relationships
    » Think about the people you've allowed into your life. Do they align with your nonnegotiables?
    » Were there red flags you ignored in the name of hope, comfort, or history?
3. Envision Your Future Goals
    » Picture your ideal relationship. What does it feel like?
    » What qualities must your future partner possess in words and consistent action?
    » Write these down as a blueprint to both manifest a relationship and protect your peace when one appears.
4. Self-Reflection: Mirror Check

THE JOURNEY

- » If you met yourself today, would you want to be in a relationship with you?
- » Are you living out the values and emotional maturity you seek in others?
- » If yes, celebrate that growth. Write down the qualities you love about yourself.
- » If not, that's okay. Awareness is the first step. Be honest about the areas you want to improve and then commit to taking intentional steps forward. You deserve to be the partner you're trying to attract.

CHAPTER 6

Crossroads

A single bad day doesn't define your whole life.
—CHRISTINA VERA

WE ALL FACE crossroads. Those moments in life when everything feels uncertain, heavy, or out of our control. Sometimes it's a sudden loss, a personal failure, a painful breakup, or a season of deep emotional exhaustion. Other times it's something bigger, like the impact of a global pandemic that disrupted everything we thought was stable. But no matter what form it takes, one thing remains true: *A single bad day does not define your entire life.*

It's easy to let one hard moment cloud your vision or convince you that you've lost your way. But even in chaos, clarity can emerge. Even in disappointment, direction can be found. Crossroads are not dead ends; they are invitations to pause, reflect, and choose a new path forward.

In this chapter, we will explore what it means to stand at the edge of uncertainty and still choose hope. You'll be reminded that your story is still unfolding, and the power to shape what comes next is already within you. No matter how heavy today feels, it's just one page in a much bigger, much more powerful story.

Let's leave fear behind and step into the crossroads with faith.

I'm learning to reprogram my thinking and embrace the truth that one bad day doesn't define my whole life. But let's be honest. It's a lot easier said than done, especially when you're still in the thick of the storm. Sometimes it's not just a bad day you are enduring but a bad *season*. A stretch of time where it feels like the ground beneath you is shifting, and everything you once felt sure of is now uncertain.

About a year ago, I walked through one of the hardest six months of my life. I was dealing with a deeply painful professional matter—one that became public. And by public, I mean *every* local news channel, newspaper, and social media platform shared the details. It was everywhere. I couldn't escape it. My health took a hit. My stress levels were sky-high. And every single day I found myself asking, "Why? Why me?"

As someone who is usually strong, confident, and ready to stand up and fight when necessary, I found myself at a loss. I didn't have the energy to defend myself. I didn't have the will. I didn't have the fight. Everything I had worked so hard to build felt like it was crumbling. Even though I knew in my heart that I had done nothing wrong, the weight of my title and position meant I had to be the face of the storm. The spokesperson. The strong one. On the inside, I felt completely alone. I began to doubt whether I was even the right person for the job.

On top of that, my physical health was unraveling. I lost a significant amount of weight. My blood pressure spiked. Relationships were strained. And just when I thought I couldn't take anything else, I discovered a lump in my left breast. Surgery followed.

Crossroads

Doctors' appointments filled my calendar. My life as I had known it had shifted dramatically.

That was a dark time. I can't sugarcoat it. But by the grace of God, the unwavering love of my family, and a few close friends who never let go of me—even when I could barely hold on to myself—I started to rebuild. Day by day. Thought by thought. Prayer by prayer. I began to remind myself of *who* I was and *whose* I was. I had to speak life back into myself. The Enemy was after my mind and my spirit. And at one point, I almost gave it to him. Almost.

In earlier chapters, we've talked about the power of relationships. But until you hit *your* version of rock-bottom, you don't truly understand just how vital those relationships are. During that storm, I didn't hear from many people. There were no check-ins, no words of encouragement. In fact, some of the only messages I received were rooted in gossip and messiness. And that silence—those absences—spoke volumes. It clarified everything. It showed me who was really in my corner and who only came around when the sun was shining.

That season also taught me invaluable lessons about business, leadership, and human nature. One of the biggest takeaways? *When people show you who they are, believe them.* Don't make excuses. Don't try to rewrite the narrative. Believe them, and then move on accordingly.

Eventually, the storm passed. But it left permanent internal scars. As I reflect now, I realize that even though I felt alone and exposed, I was *never* truly alone. And maybe I *was* on display, but perhaps not just for ridicule. Maybe, just maybe, I was on display to inspire someone else. Someone who needed to see what resilience looked like. Someone who needed to witness survival in real time.

Because here's what I know now: We are bigger than the battles we face. Every test has the potential to become a testimony. That truth doesn't erase the pain, and it certainly doesn't make the

THE JOURNEY

journey easy. But it offers hope. And that hope is what will carry you to the other side.

So if you're still in your storm, hear me when I say this: Stay grounded in who you are. Stay poised. Stay humble. Don't let the world see you fold. And if you need to cry? Go home, let it out, release the pain—but then get back up. Stand tall. Return as the warrior you are. Because you *will* get through this. And when you do, you'll carry wisdom, strength, and grace that only a storm like that could teach you. There was purpose in it, even if you couldn't see it at the time. There was meaning. And there was a version of you waiting on the other side who emerged stronger, wiser, and more grounded than ever before.

One of the hardest but most necessary lessons I learned during that season was to release the expectations I had placed on people. I expected support. I expected empathy. I expected phone calls, check-ins, prayers, or even just a "How are you doing?" But what I came to realize is that expectations can become silent contracts we hold against people who never agreed to sign them. And while disappointment is valid, staying stuck in it only robs you of your peace. I had to choose to stop replaying the names of those who didn't show up and start reclaiming the space in my mind that those expectations were occupying. Protecting my peace meant accepting people where they were, not where I hoped they'd be. And it also meant loving myself enough to set boundaries—emotional and spiritual—that safeguarded my healing.

While many were silent, a few showed up—consistently, quietly, lovingly. And I don't take that for granted. Sometimes it was a simple text saying, "I'm praying for you," or a call that didn't ask for details but simply offered presence. There's something sacred about people who don't need to know the whole story to show up for you. They love you in the dark without needing to shine a light on your pain for their own comfort or curiosity. Their presence reminded me that love doesn't always come in grand gestures. Sometimes it's a steady whisper that says, "You are not alone." Those people became anchors in the storm, and they are the ones I will cherish forever. Because when I had nothing to offer, they showed up anyway.

In the quiet of my healing, I realized I had a choice to make. I could carry my story with resentment, or I could carry it with purpose. Sharing from a place of hurt would only reopen the wounds. But sharing from a place of healing meant I could turn my pain into power. That shift changed everything. It's not that the scars disappeared—they didn't. But they no longer dictated how I showed up in the world. I stopped bleeding on people and instead began offering the bandages that helped me heal. Now when I speak about what I went through, I do it with clarity, not chaos. I want people to feel hope, not pity. My story no longer controls me. Instead, I carry it as a badge of resilience, not resentment. And when the time is right, I hope you will share your story. Not from the wound but from the healing. Because someone out there needs to know that survival isn't just possible; it's promised.

I want to share with you the story of how I navigated one of the most difficult crossroads in my professional life. At the time, I was serving as a leader in an organization whose mission was to serve minorities and uplift underserved communities. I saw it as my dream job—a place where I could help others make their dreams come true and take steps toward their own version of the American Dream.

But then I was met with opposition. And not from strangers or outsiders, but from people I trusted, people I had confided in. The shift was subtle at first, but day by day, the tension grew heavier. I couldn't understand why. I started questioning myself and my work. I prayed for clarity. I asked God to help me see what I couldn't.

Then one day during a meeting, it all became painfully clear. The people making my days so difficult were acting out of fear. Their jobs were on the line, and they believed that by pushing me out, they might secure their own positions as the organization underwent restructuring. I was stunned. Hurt. But in that moment, I understood. Their actions weren't about me. They were about survival.

I tried to stay strong. I focused on doing my job with excellence and did my best to ignore the toxicity. But it eventually became too much. I realized I was sacrificing my peace to stay in a place that no longer nurtured me. Around that time, I was approached about a new opportunity—one that aligned with my passions and offered a more collaborative, youthful, and growth-oriented environment. I applied. I got the job. Still, I hesitated. This had been my dream. I didn't want to walk away from it.

But then something happened that made the decision crystal clear. I won't go into details, but I will say this: When your spirit has told you to leave, when God has made it abundantly clear and you continue to stay, you invite unnecessary pain. God had already opened another door. I just needed to walk through it. So I did. That day, I chose peace. I didn't give two weeks' notice, which was something I had never done in my entire career, and I've been working since I was fifteen years old. I simply said, "Thank you. Today is my last day."

I knew in my soul that the environment no longer served my growth, my peace, or my future. And as hard as it was to walk away from something I once loved deeply, I don't regret it. It was the right decision. In fact, up to that point in my life, it was the best decision I had made. It is true that everything works out for our own good. Even if at that time we can't fully see it.

Today, if I face a change or a hard moment, I pause, reflect and react. I pause to take a moment to evaluate what is happening, focusing on the facts and trying to remove emotions. I reflect that to this point all the good and not so good have worked for my own good. God has never forsaken me. I react by using one of the tools of my toolbox to recenter myself and decide on my next best step. I don't have to figure it all out in that moment, just focus the next best step. What is the next best step for your current situation?

HOW TO NAVIGATE A BAD DAY OR BAD SEASON

When life gets heavy—whether it's a tough day or an extended season of hardship—your mindset becomes your lifeline. It's easy to spiral into frustration, self-doubt, or hopelessness when nothing seems to be going right. But how you *respond in* those moments is more powerful than what's happening around you. Bad days are inevitable. Seasons of difficulty are part of the human experience. But neither one is permanent. And neither has the authority to define your worth, your purpose, or your future. Start by acknowledging how you feel without shame. You don't have to pretend you're okay when you're not. Give yourself permission to feel, process, and pause. But don't unpack and live there.

Hard days don't mean you are failing. Challenging seasons don't mean you've lost your way or missed your purpose. Sometimes the struggle isn't a sign that you're off track; it's evidence that you're *in process*. Growth doesn't always feel graceful. In fact, some of the most transformative seasons begin in discomfort, confusion, and stillness.

Just like a seed must be buried before it can rise, your next level often starts in the dark where things feel uncertain, unfamiliar, and hard to explain. But beneath the surface, something is taking root. Strength is being built. Character is being refined. Vision is being sharpened. So when it feels like nothing is moving, remind yourself that the soil is working. Your foundation is forming. You are not stuck; you're being *prepared*.

And when in doubt, look back. You've survived every hard day before this one. You've walked through what you once thought would break you. And yet, you're still standing. That alone is proof of your resilience. Proof that even in the tension of waiting, in the stretch of growth, and in the silence of uncertainty, you are becoming. Hold on. Keep going. Because what's being planted during this season may just be the harvest you've been praying for.

Here are some practical ways to navigate a bad day or challenging season:

1. *Reset, Don't Retreat*: Take a step back, breathe, and give yourself space to reset. A pause is not the same as giving up.
2. *Reframe the Narrative*: Ask yourself, "What is this moment here to teach me?" Even in pain, there is perspective to be gained.
3. *Lean on Your Tools*: Prayer, journaling, movement, therapy, a trusted friend—use what grounds you and reminds you of who you are.
4. *Focus on What You Can Control:* You may not be able to change the situation, but you can control your response, your thoughts, and your environment.
5. *Celebrate Small Wins*: On hard days, getting out of bed, answering that email, or taking a walk counts as a win. Progress is still progress, even when it's quiet.
6. *Extend Yourself Grace*: You are allowed to not have it all together. Healing, growth, and clarity often come in waves. Be gentle with yourself in the process.
7. *Speak Truth to Yourself*: Replace self-defeating thoughts

with affirmations that ground you in truth: "This is temporary. I've survived hard things before. I am still worthy."
8. *Zoom Out*: Look at the bigger picture. One season does not define your entire journey. Storms are real, but so is the sun after them.
9. *Practice Emotional Boundaries*: Protect your peace. Limit exposure to negative influences, gossip, or energy-draining people while you heal.
10. *Gratitude as a Weapon*: Even in the dark, look for light. Write down three things each day that remind you life is good. Gratitude reframes the storm.
11. *Ask for Support, Then Receive It*: You don't have to carry it alone. Let your trusted circle pour into you. Vulnerability is not weakness; it's wisdom.
12. *Remind Yourself That This Isn't the End*: This difficult moment is a chapter, not the whole book. The version of you that will come out of this—wiser, stronger, more compassionate—is worth holding on for.

BUILDING RESILIENCE: INNER STRENGTH THAT LASTS

Resilience isn't about having it all together. It's not about suppressing your emotions or pretending everything's okay when it's not. True resilience is about *knowing* that life will shake you and choosing to stand back up anyway. It's the ability to bend without breaking, to feel deeply and still move forward, and to keep going even when the path ahead is unclear.

Resilience is the quiet strength within you—the kind that doesn't always roar but refuses to quit. It's built through experience, forged in adversity, and strengthened each time you choose growth over giving up. But resilience isn't something you simply "have." It's something you *build*. And building it requires intention.

It means creating internal systems (mental, emotional, spiritual) that allow you to bounce back when life gets hard, such as:

- Self-awareness to recognize your triggers, limitations, and needs.
- Healthy coping mechanisms that don't just numb the pain but help you process it.
- Support networks of people who uplift and challenge you.
- Daily habits that restore your energy and protect your peace.

Resilience is also about giving yourself permission to rest without labeling it as weakness. It's recognizing that healing and strength can coexist. You can cry and still be courageous. You can pause and still be powerful. When you build resilience, you're not just preparing for the storms; you're building a foundation that keeps you grounded no matter what comes. Because resilience isn't about being untouched by hardship. It's about being *transformed* by it—stronger, wiser, and more rooted than ever before.

Here's how you can build the resilience muscle over time:

1. **Accept That Life Will Test You.** Resilience begins with acceptance. Life will throw curveballs—some unfair, some unexpected. Resilient people don't pretend it's easy; they prepare for the hard, hope for the best, and stay anchored in who they are.
2. **Learn from the Low Points.** Every storm leaves behind lessons; some painful, some powerful. Take time to reflect on what each challenge is teaching you. Did you learn something about trust? Boundaries? Yourself? That's growth.
3. **Develop a Resilience Routine.** Whether it's journaling, prayer, morning walks, deep breathing, or

therapy—establish a rhythm that strengthens your mind, body, and soul. During this time, write about the things you have accomplished or overcome. There will be a time when you may need to remind yourself that you have overcome hard things! You don't build resilience in the moment of crisis. You build it in the moments between.
4. **Keep Showing Up.** Even if you're tired. Even if you're unsure. Showing up for yourself day after day is how you prove to your spirit that you won't abandon it.
5. **Focus on Progress, Not Perfection.** Resilient people don't strive to never fall. They strive to rise with more wisdom each time. Your bounce-back may not be instant, but every small step forward is still movement.
6. **Protect What Fuels You.** Your energy is your lifeline. Protect your peace. Guard your time. Prioritize people and environments that pour back into you, not drain you.
7. **Remind Yourself Who You Are.** When life tries to make you forget your power, resilience is the inner voice that says: *You've made it through worse. You're still standing. You're still becoming. Remember who made you in His image.*

MOVE FORWARD WITH CONFIDENCE

There comes a moment in everyone's journey where you're faced with a choice: Stay in the comfort of what you've always known, or take a step into the unknown. Let's be honest: Comfort is tempting. It feels safe, predictable, and easy to navigate. But growth doesn't live in comfort zones. It lives in the stretch, in the uncertainty, in the brave moments when you choose change over fear.

We've had several of those moments, but one that stands out vividly was during the COVID-19 pandemic. Like so many others, our world shifted overnight. Plans were canceled, routines were disrupted, and the normalcy we had relied on evaporated

THE JOURNEY

almost overnight. We had two choices: freeze or adapt. That season forced us to dig deep, to think creatively, and to find new ways to serve, lead, and thrive. It was uncomfortable, yes, but it was also transformational. What we thought would break us actually built a version of us that we didn't know we had access to.

That's the thing about change. It often shows up uninvited, but it always brings an opportunity if we're willing to receive it. Embracing the unknown doesn't mean you won't be afraid. It means you choose to move forward *despite* the fear. When you stretch beyond your familiar surroundings, you make room for new relationships, new skills, and new perspectives. We've learned that sometimes the risk isn't in taking the leap; it's in staying stuck.

Adversity is one of life's greatest teachers. It strips away distractions and forces you to confront what really matters. The pandemic, for example, revealed weaknesses in systems, relationships, and habits. But it also revealed strength, resilience, and innovation. We saw people pivot, create, and reimagine. We did the same. We built new programs, explored different platforms, and discovered capacities within ourselves that we never would've uncovered without the push of discomfort.

Opportunities don't always arrive with a formal invitation. Sometimes they look like detours. Sometimes they're disguised as setbacks. But if you remain open—if you keep your heart, mind, and spirit flexible—you'll find that life often exceeds your expectations.

I've learned to ask myself, "What else is possible?" That simple question has opened doors I didn't even know existed. But change alone isn't enough. To truly move forward, you need confidence in your ability to handle whatever comes next, even when the path is unclear. And confidence doesn't appear overnight. It's built through small, consistent action.

Crossroads

Setting realistic goals has been key in helping me navigate seasons of change. When everything feels uncertain, it's grounding to focus on what's in your control. I break big dreams into bite-sized steps, and each small win reminds me that I'm capable. That progress—even if it's slow—keeps me motivated.

And I've learned to celebrate along the way. Not just the big wins, but the quiet ones too. The days I didn't give up. The emails I finally sent. The self-care I prioritized. Every step counts. Acknowledging progress reinforces a mindset of growth and keeps the fire inside lit.

Visualization has also become a powerful tool in my toolbox. I take time to picture where I'm headed—how it looks, how it feels, who I'm becoming. That mental rehearsal helps me stay focused, especially when doubt tries to creep in. Seeing the finish line in my mind helps me stay committed when the work gets tough.

Life is going to shift. Seasons will change. Challenges will come. But if you embrace the unknown, stay open to new possibilities, and keep moving forward with intention and confidence, there is nothing you can't overcome.

You're not just surviving change; you're shaping your future through it. You're not just surviving change; you're shaping your future through it. Every challenge you face, every pivot you make, and every moment of uncertainty you endure is not just something to get through—it's an opportunity to intentionally build the life you envision. Change, though uncomfortable, is the soil where your next level of growth is planted. It refines your character, strengthens your resilience, and reveals possibilities you might not have seen otherwise. Instead of fearing the unknown, you are learning to meet it with purpose and vision, using it as a tool to carve out a future that reflects your true potential. You are not a passive participant in your story; you are the author, and change is one of your greatest co-writers.

THE JOURNEY

FROM SETBACK TO SETUP
As this chapter concludes, take a deep breath and give yourself permission to reset. Hard days come, but they always pass. What matters most is how you choose to respond, grow, and realign when they do. The goal isn't to avoid difficulty altogether; it's to build the strength and perspective to move *through* it with wisdom and grace.

A bad day is just a *day*, not your destiny. It's one page in the story, not the whole book. These moments, as challenging as they may be, are temporary chapters designed to teach, shape, and prepare you for what's ahead. When you shift your perspective and lean into the lesson rather than resisting the discomfort, you unlock your power to transform adversity into alignment.

Every obstacle becomes an invitation. Every challenge offers a chance to rise. Every setback opens the door for your next breakthrough. You are not defined by your worst day. You are shaped by what you choose to do next. So take this time to reflect, reset, and reconnect with your power. Let resilience become your rhythm. Let perspective lead the way. And most of all, remind yourself daily that even on the hardest days, *you are still becoming*.

Your resilience isn't built in the mountaintop moments. It's built in the quiet decisions to keep going. To try again. To believe—*even here*—there's still something greater ahead.

You've come this far. Keep climbing. Your next breakthrough might just be one choice away.

♦ Christina
🦋 Maylin

PAUSE, REFLECT, AND REACT

From Obstacles to Opportunities

Take time to reflect on these strategies and begin weaving them into your daily life. Remember, a bad day is just that—a day, not your destiny. It's a temporary moment in a much larger journey. When you learn to shift your perspective and embrace the lesson hidden within the challenge, you give yourself the power to rise with resilience and walk forward with grace. Every obstacle becomes an opportunity. Every setback is a setup for your next breakthrough.

Remember: One bad day doesn't write the whole story. By reflecting, staying open, and leaning into resilience, you begin to transform adversity into alignment. Use this space to reconnect with your power and step confidently into what's next.

1. **Revisit a Recent Challenge.** Think back to a recent tough day or season. What happened? How did it impact you emotionally, mentally, or physically? Be honest with yourself, then reflect: What did this experience teach you about yourself, others, or life?
2. **Name Your Resilience Tools.** Write down the mindset shifts or strategies that help you stay grounded during difficult moments. What practices—like deep breathing, gratitude, prayer, journaling, or unplugging—can you turn to when life gets heavy? How can you begin to strengthen your resilience day by day?
3. **Embrace Something New.** Identify an area in your life where you've been hesitant to try something unfamiliar— maybe a new opportunity, a fresh routine, or a different mindset. Journal about what's possible if you say yes.

THE JOURNEY

What growth, joy, or discovery could be waiting on the other side of your comfort zone?

CHAPTER 7

A Pathway to Progress

*Progress is not a destination, but a journey of
persistence, courage, and unyielding faith.
Keep moving forward one step at a time.*

—MAYLIN SAMBOIS

PROGRESS ISN'T ALWAYS loud. It doesn't always look like big wins, overnight success, or picture-perfect milestones. More often, it's quiet. Subtle. Found in the small, intentional steps you take when no one is watching. It's built in the days when you feel like giving up but choose to show up anyway.

This chapter is about honoring the journey, not just the outcome. It's about recognizing that forward movement is still progress, even when it feels slow. It's the reminder that healing, growth, and purpose don't follow a straight path. There are detours. Delays. Moments when you wonder if you're even moving at all.

But every time you choose to try again, every time you realign, recommit, or simply breathe through the hard parts—you are building momentum. You are laying the bricks of your future, one step at a time. Progress doesn't require perfection. It only asks for your *presence*. Let's walk this path together with grace, intention, and a renewed belief that what's ahead is worth every step.

Fifteen years ago, Maylin and I each independently signed up for a women's leadership program in our city. Ironically, on the day the program was set to begin, we both contemplated canceling, feeling like we didn't "have time." But in the end, we both chose to show up—and that decision changed everything. It's where we first met, and the rest became our story. The Women's Leadership Program for Latinas was more than a meeting point; it was a vehicle that set Maylin and me on a course toward a higher purpose. It wasn't merely a chance encounter or networking opportunity. It was a catalyst, a launching pad that connected us to something deeper—our purpose, our calling, and, ultimately, our destiny. In the busyness of life, we often forget that such experiences are not just coincidental but intentional. They are moments where preparation meets opportunity, guiding us toward the future we're meant to shape.

This program did more than gather women with similar backgrounds; it became a space where we began to understand the power of our stories, our heritage, and the roles we were destined to play as leaders. We often underestimate the value of intentional spaces like these, thinking they are just one-off events, but they can hold immense power. This was not just a series of workshops or sessions; it was an initiation into a journey that many of us had unconsciously prepared for. It became the moment we began to see the path forward not just for ourselves but for our communities.

A Pathway to Progress

What we experienced wasn't by chance; it was deliberate. The women who gathered in that program did not stumble into leadership by accident. We had all shown up with intention. The very act of showing up allowed the program to be a vehicle for change, for growth, and for transformation. It became the place where potential met opportunity, where preparation met purpose.

In life, we often move through the motions—fulfilling responsibilities, checking off tasks, and managing obligations. But when we intentionally position ourselves in spaces of growth, we create opportunities for our trajectories to shift. The Women's Leadership Program wasn't just about networking or professional development; it was about stepping into our own leadership potential and claiming the space we were meant to occupy.

At times, we overlook the moments that push us closer to our destiny because they don't always come with fanfare or recognition. But this program showed us that destiny is something we must actively pursue, and it doesn't always come easily or on our terms. It requires preparation, courage, and the willingness to show up, even when it's hard.

It's easy to forget how pivotal these experiences are in the busyness of our lives. But what we must remember is that they are not random. They are divinely orchestrated moments where preparation meets opportunity, where the trajectory of our lives changes. And when we look back, we realize these experiences were milestones—turning points—where we began to shape our futures.

What set this program apart was the sense of shared purpose among the women who participated. It was about collective impact. Each of us came to understand that our leadership was not just for our own benefit but for the benefit of those who came before us, those who stood alongside us, and those who would come after us.

The Women's Leadership Program (also known to us as the Latina Mentoring Academy) created a space where Latina women could gather, learn, and lead. This six-month program became a bridge between where we were at the beginning of the cohort and where we were destined to go. The relationships we formed, the lessons we learned, and the visions we created during this time laid the foundation for the trajectories of our lives—personally, professionally, and within our community. I often reflect on where I'd be if I (or Maylin) hadn't shown up for that cohort. It's a powerful reminder that showing up, even when you are feeling uncertain or uncomfortable, can shift the entire trajectory of your life. The power of presence is real, and sometimes that one decision to show up is the beginning of everything. It's easy to underestimate the impact of simply being in the room—whether it's stepping into a new opportunity, sitting at a table you once felt unqualified for, or choosing to face a challenge instead of avoiding it. Presence is more than physical; it's a declaration to yourself and the world that you are willing to be seen, to be counted, and to participate in the life you're building. Often, the doors that open, the connections that are made, and the clarity that emerges come only after you take that first courageous step to be present. Transformation doesn't always announce itself with grand gestures—it often begins quietly, in the simple but powerful act of showing up.

THE POWER OF SHOWING UP

Are you intentionally positioning yourself to meet your destiny? Think about that for a moment. Every decision you make, every place you go, and every time you step into new territory, you are actively shaping the future version of yourself. It's easy to get caught up in external accomplishments (titles, goals, recognition), but the most meaningful transformation happens when you respond to the quiet call within. The whisper that says, *There is more for you.*

Showing up is more than just being present; it's about aligning with purpose. It's saying yes when everything in you wants to retreat. It's choosing growth over comfort, clarity over chaos, and courage over convenience. Showing up is what bridges the gap between where you are and where you're meant to be.

Showing up isn't always easy. It's often inconvenient and comes with vulnerability, risk, and sometimes even rejection. There are days when doubt feels louder than purpose. Moments when fear convinces us we're not ready. Times when busyness becomes a distraction from our own alignment. Yet it is in these very moments that showing up matters the most.

Think about the opportunities you almost didn't take. What if you hadn't said yes to that program, event, or chance meeting? What if fear, exhaustion, or uncertainty had kept you from being in the room? That one step, that one yes might have been the divine connection point—the moment that shifted your entire trajectory. Every time you show up, you create space for alignment, growth, and possibility.

Showing up also deepens the relationship we have with ourselves. It builds self-trust. Every time you honor a commitment, walk into a room feeling unsure, or pursue something greater than where you are, you affirm that you're worthy of the life you envision. You begin to believe in your own capacity to evolve.

The people you meet, the lessons you learn, and the confidence you gain are not accidental happenings. These moments are divinely orchestrated and activated by your willingness to be present. And it's often not just about what you receive, but what you *bring* to the space. Your energy, your voice, your story—they matter. Someone in the room might be waiting for a word only you can give. Sometimes showing up isn't just about you; it's about who is watching you rise.

So ask yourself: "Where is life calling me to show up more fully?" Maybe it's in your relationships, your purpose, your healing, or your leadership. Maybe it's simply showing up for yourself each morning, believing that you are worthy of the vision planted in your heart.

THE JOURNEY

You don't have to have it all figured out to take the first step. But you do have to be willing to move. To trust. To say yes, again and again. Because the truth is, your destiny is often waiting on the other side of your decision to show up. When you lean into the unknown with faith rather than fear, you create momentum—and momentum is where the magic begins. Each small, intentional step sends a signal to the world, to your future self, and to every opportunity meant for you that you are ready. Doors you didn't even know existed start to open. People and resources begin to align. Your confidence grows, not because you know every answer, but because you've proven to yourself that you're willing to keep walking forward. Growth doesn't require perfection—it requires movement, heart, and a willingness to believe that where you are today is only the beginning of where you're meant to go.

HOW TO SHOW UP, EVEN WHEN IT'S HARD

How do you show up for yourself, even on the days when your energy is low, when your spirit feels heavy, or when your confidence is barely holding on? That question is more than rhetorical. It's a lived experience, especially for women of color, whose leadership journeys are often laced with navigating systemic barriers, cultural expectations, and the invisible labor of simply being seen.

Showing up isn't about having all the answers. It's not about being polished, perfect, or put together. It's about *resilience*. It's about choosing to be present, to take a step forward, even when your knees are trembling. It's trusting that each act of showing up is a seed planted for your future. That even if the outcome is uncertain, the decision to try is a declaration of belief in yourself.

We've had days where showing up felt nearly impossible. Days when the weight of responsibilities, self-doubt, and fatigue made me want to retreat and stay hidden. But what we've each learned is that showing up doesn't always mean stepping into the spotlight. Sometimes it means looking in the mirror and whispering, "I'm

A Pathway to Progress

still here." It means replying to the email you've been avoiding, attending the meeting even if your voice shakes, or simply getting out of bed and choosing to face the day.

For women of color in particular, showing up is often an act of resistance. It's a bold refusal to be erased, diminished, or silenced. When you show up—despite what society says you can't do, despite what history has tried to limit—you reclaim your power. You become the author of your own narrative.

You don't have to wait until you feel ready to begin. Readiness is often a myth that convinces us to delay our dreams. Confidence grows through action, not before it. The truth is, your destiny doesn't require perfection; it requires presence. It requires your voice, your perspective, and your experience.

Every time you show up, you're building a muscle. You're proving to yourself that fear won't have the final say. You're affirming that your dreams are worth the discomfort. That you are worth the effort.

So how do you show up when it's hard? You take one step. Then another. You remind yourself why you started. You give yourself grace when you fall short. You ask for help when you need it. You look in the mirror and say, "Not today, fear."

And if no one claps for you, then clap for yourself. Showing up for yourself is one of the greatest acts of self-love you will ever commit to. It tells the world—and more importantly, it tells *you*—that you matter. That your story matters. That your presence carries weight.

So when the day feels heavy and the mountain looks too high, remember this: You don't have to do it all. You just have to show up. Imperfectly. Afraid. Tired. That's enough. And that's powerful.

EMBRACING IMPERFECT PROGRESS

One of the hardest truths to accept on the journey to growth is this: *Progress is rarely linear.* We often expect a clear path, one with consistent wins, upward momentum, and visible results. But real progress? It's often winding. Uncomfortable. Full of starts, stops, and unexpected turns.

After you've shown up for yourself—especially after pushing past fear or resistance—it can feel frustrating when things don't immediately fall into place. You may find yourself hitting emotional walls, questioning your progress, or wondering if you're moving at all. But here's what you have to remember: *Setbacks don't erase forward movement.*

Progress is not perfection. It's not about getting everything right; it's about *getting back up*. It's about learning through the messy moments, showing grace to yourself during the plateaus, and recognizing that even the pauses and pivots have a purpose. Some days will feel like giant leaps. Others will feel like tiny, trembling steps. And there will be days when simply choosing to rest, breathe, or not give up is the *bravest act of progress* you can make.

Real progress includes these elements:

- Saying no to what no longer aligns, even when it's hard.
- Taking a break without labeling yourself as lazy.
- Asking for help instead of suffering in silence.
- Reassessing your goals when life shifts unexpectedly.

Growth isn't always about doing more. Sometimes it's about doing things *differently*—with more intention, clarity, and compassion. Give yourself permission to evolve at your own pace. Your journey is not a race; it's a *becoming*.

You're allowed to stumble. You're allowed to stretch. You're even allowed to outgrow old versions of yourself more than once. Growth is not a straight line—it's messy, layered, and often uncomfortable. But every misstep, every uncomfortable stretch, and every quiet evolution is part of the journey. So keep showing up. Keep planting seeds. Even when it feels slow, even when it feels like no one sees the work you're doing, trust that your consistency is doing the quiet, invisible work of transformation. Roots grow deep before anything blooms above the surface. Your patience, your persistence, and your willingness to keep going—especially on the days when it would be easier to quit—are building a foundation stronger than you can yet see. Stay faithful to the process; your harvest is closer than you think.

CONSISTENCY OVER INTENSITY

In a world that glorifies hustle culture, overnight success, and quick transformations, it's easy to fall into the trap of thinking that progress must be loud, fast, or extreme. But real, sustainable growth? It's built through *consistency* not intensity.

Many people burn out not because they lack motivation, but because they try to change everything at once. They go all in for a short burst and then fizzle out when life inevitably gets hard or the results don't come quickly enough. The truth is, transformation doesn't require a massive overhaul of your life in a single day. What it requires is *showing up*, again and again, with small, intentional steps.

There is power in the compound effect of daily discipline. One aligned action, repeated over time, carries more weight than sporadic bursts of energy. Think of discipline as creating a pattern—a steady rhythm that your future can dance to. Your habits form the architecture of your progress, laying brick by brick the foundation of the life you're building. Even the smallest shifts—a few minutes of focus, a single brave decision, a daily act of self-care—stack up in ways that are invisible at first but undeniable over time. Momentum isn't created by doing everything all at once; it's created by doing the right things, the intentional things, over and over until they transform from effort into instinct. Success is rarely about giant leaps—it's about the quiet, committed steps you take when no one is watching, trusting that every small investment is pulling you closer to the life you're meant to live. While motivation can inspire you to start, it's discipline that will carry you across the finish line.

BUILD YOUR PROGRESS RHYTHM

Here are a few simple strategies to help you focus on sustainable consistency:

- **Morning Affirmations:** Start your day with a few intentional statements that ground you in your purpose and reframe your mindset.
  - » *Example:* "I honor slow progress because I trust where I am headed."
- **Weekly Reflection:** Set aside ten to fifteen minutes each week to check in with yourself and ask: "What worked this week? Where did I feel out of alignment? What small adjustment can I make next week to move closer to my goals?"
- **Nonnegotiable Habits:** Choose *one small thing* you commit to daily, no matter how busy or drained you feel. It could be journaling for five minutes, moving your body, drinking water first thing in the morning, or praying before bed. This daily anchor builds confidence and creates trust with yourself.
- **Celebrate Small Wins:** Make it a habit to acknowledge what's *working*, even if it feels minor. Progress deserves to be seen, especially the quiet kind.

Intensity fades. Life gets busy. Motivation fluctuates. But consistency? *That's what builds legacy.* So instead of trying to change your life overnight, try committing to one aligned step today, and again tomorrow. Let consistency be your power move. Let it be the quiet revolution that reshapes your path, one faithful step at a time.

REDEFINING SUCCESS ON YOUR OWN TERMS

One of the most liberating things you can do on your journey to progress is to *redefine what success means to you*. For too long, many of us have measured our worth and value through someone else's lens—chasing titles, timelines, or expectations that were never truly ours to begin with. But real success is deeply personal. It's not just about what you achieve; it's about *how* you feel while you're achieving it. It's about alignment. Fulfillment. Purpose.

True success is found in meaning and purpose It might look like launching your dream business. Or it might look like finally creating boundaries, choosing rest, or breaking generational cycles. For some, it's earning more money. For others, it's having more time with family. There is *no universal definition of success*, and there shouldn't be.

As we work through the process of redefining success, we must also give ourselves permission to release the pressure to constantly perform, prove, or achieve just to feel worthy. The comparison trap is real—and dangerous. Social media, family expectations, cultural norms, and even your inner critic can pressure you to believe you're falling behind everyone else. But you are *not* behind. You're on your *own* timeline. And your journey isn't meant to mirror anyone else's.

Let go of the myth that you must "have it all together" by a certain age or stage. Let go of the silent scorecard you've been carrying around that says you're only worthy if you're checking all the boxes. That version of success will keep you performing, not progressing. Progress is when peace becomes your metric. When alignment matters more than applause. When you stop trying to impress the world and start choosing what *fulfills* you

Success loses its meaning when it's based on someone else's expectations. That's why it's so important to pause, reflect, and ask yourself the deeper questions: *What does a successful life truly feel like to me?* Not what it looks like on paper or social media.

THE JOURNEY

Is your definition of success rooted in your values, or in a narrative that was handed to you? Many of us have adopted goals that weren't ours to begin with—standards set by our families, culture, society, or even social media. We end up pursuing degrees, careers, lifestyles, and timelines that were never aligned with our true calling. And then we wonder why we still feel unfulfilled, even when it looks like we've "made it."

This is your invitation to check in with yourself and ask:

- "What goals are *mine* born from my passion, purpose, and truth?"
- "What goals have I been chasing because they were expected of me?"
- "Am I creating a life that honors my peace, or one that just earns applause?"

When you start measuring your progress by *internal alignment*—by how grounded, free, and purposeful you feel—everything begins to shift. You stop striving for validation and start living from a place of clarity. You stop performing for acceptance and begin showing up in full expression. True success doesn't need to be loud. It doesn't have to be flashy. Sometimes, it's soft. Sometimes, it looks like rest. Sometimes, it's simply being able to say, "I like who I am becoming." Because *real* success is when:

- Your soul feels seen.
- Your values are protected.
- Your actions reflect your purpose, even if no one else is clapping.

This is your life. Your timeline. Your journey. You get to define what thriving looks and feels like for you. You are not only worthy

A Pathway to Progress

when you succeed. You are worthy while you're learning, healing, and growing. Your value isn't tied to how much you produce, how fast you move, or how perfectly you perform. You are allowed to be in process. You are allowed to evolve at your own pace. Even when progress isn't loud or visible to others, it's still happening. Some of your greatest breakthroughs will come in the quiet moments—the shift in mindset, the decision to keep going, the private victory no one else sees. That matters.

Give yourself permission to breathe. To be. To move forward on *your* terms, in *your* time, and in *your* truth. Let go of timelines that don't belong to you. Release the pressure to perform for validation or approval. Reclaim your definition of success—one that honors your values, your energy, and your vision. You don't have to earn your worth. You already are enough.

Writing this chapter alongside Christina was an invitation to reflect on the kind of progress that doesn't always come with fanfare—but it is deeply transformational, nonetheless. The title, "*A Pathway to Progress*" is about what it means to keep showing up for ourselves and others, even when things feel unclear, uncomfortable, or incomplete.

Through the lens of our time in the Latina Mentoring Academy and the spaces we continue to grow in, I've learned that true progress often happens in the quiet moments—the ones where we choose grace over guilt, courage over comfort, and presence over perfection. This chapter holds pieces of that journey: the vulnerability we shared, the tears we shed, the laughter we needed, and the reminders we gave each other to just keep going.

More than anything, this chapter is meant to be read like a love letter for every woman learning to trust herself again, to honor her own pace, and to find power in imperfection. Progress is about

THE JOURNEY

taking one brave step after another, having one honest conversation at a time, and giving yourself a daily, gentle reminder that says, "I am becoming, and that's more than enough."

⧫ Christina
🦋 Maylin

PAUSE, REFLECT, AND REACT

Progress in Presence

PAUSE

Take a deep breath. Give yourself permission to stop striving and simply *be*. Let go of the pressure to have it all figured out. You're here, and that means you're already progressing.

REFLECT

- What does progress look and feel like to you in this season?
- In what areas of your life have you grown, even if it's a small change?
- Are there areas where you've been chasing someone else's version of success?
- What's one belief about success or progress that you're ready to release?
- Reflect on a pivotal moment in your life where you chose to show up despite uncertainty or fear. What motivated you to take that step, and how did it change your trajectory?
- Think about an area of your life where you feel called to show up more fully. What intentional steps can you take to create space for growth and alignment?
- In what ways do you practice resilience when life feels overwhelming?
- Write down a personal mantra or affirmation that reminds you to keep going. Save it in your phone, write it on a sticky note, or tuck it into your purse—somewhere you'll see it when you need it most.

REACT
- Write down one small aligned action you can take this week that supports *your* definition of progress. This might be setting a boundary, creating a new habit, giving yourself a break, or saying no to something that drains you.
- Speak this over yourself: "I honor where I am. I trust where I am going."

CHAPTER 8

Who Do You See in the Mirror?

> *The reflection you see is not just who you are, but who you choose to become. Dare to see greatness, even in your imperfections, and let that vision guide your path.*
> —MAYLIN SAMBOIS

WHEN YOU LOOK in the mirror, who do you truly see? Don't focus on the surface reflection but on the person beneath—the real you. For many of us, the person staring back isn't aligned with who we know we're capable of becoming. It's easy to get lost in the demands of life, forgetting the promises we've made to ourselves along the way. The path to reclaiming the real you starts with seeing yourself clearly and committing to rediscovering your authentic self.

So many of us go through life on autopilot. We check the boxes, fulfill the roles, and meet expectations set by others. But somewhere along the way we lose touch with the version of ourselves we promised to become. The reflection grows dimmer, and the voice within gets quieter. We forget that *becoming* is a choice. That clarity comes when we stop running from our reflection and begin to have an honest conversation with it.

This chapter is about returning to yourself. It's about reclaiming your reflection—not the one filtered through other people's opinions, past failures, or present insecurities—but the one that reflects your highest, most authentic self.

WHO ARE YOU?

This question may sound simple, but it goes far beyond labels like career titles, roles in relationships, or external achievements. Who are you at your core? The answer to this question shapes how you show up in the world. When you look in the mirror, who do you truly see?

Not just your face, your body, or your expression, but the essence behind the eyes. The version of you that holds your dreams, your doubts, your resilience, your regrets. It's easy to stare at our reflection and only notice the imperfections—what's missing, what's broken, what we think we should have become by now. But the mirror doesn't lie. It reveals not only where you are, but hints at who you're meant to be—if you're brave enough to look closely.

This is where the transformation begins. The moment you decide to reprogram your life is the moment you step into a new identity, one that reflects your true worth and power. Reprogramming doesn't happen overnight; it starts with a shift in perspective and intention.

WHEN I LOOK IN THE MIRROR, WHO DO I TRULY SEE?

Before we could step into who we were meant to be, we had to get honest about who we were in that moment. That kind of reflection

Who Do You See in the Mirror?

doesn't happen overnight—it requires courage, vulnerability, and a willingness to face ourselves without the filters. Together, we asked the tough questions, peeled back the layers, and held space for the truths we each uncovered. One question echoed for both of us: *When I look in the mirror, who do I truly see?*

---◆---

I see a woman who has learned how to lead with grace, even when the weight of responsibility felt unbearable. I see someone who has walked through storms publicly and privately, who has been scrutinized, misunderstood, celebrated, yet still chose to show up. I see a mother who wakes up daily carrying not just her own dreams, but the hopes of little eyes watching closely. I see a nonprofit leader who dared to build a table for others when none was offered to her. I see an author who turned personal pain into words that help others heal.

But more than anything, I see someone who is still becoming.

There was a time I believed the reflection in the mirror had to be perfect in order to be powerful. Now I understand that power comes from presence, not perfection. I've made peace with the fact that growth is messy. Leadership is hard. Motherhood is humbling. And purpose will stretch you beyond anything comfort ever could.

When I look in the mirror, I don't just see a title or a to-do list. I see a woman who knows that every version of herself (past, present, and future) matters. I see someone who has learned how to keep her heart soft, her boundaries strong, and her vision clear. I see a fighter. A vessel. A mirror for others who need to be reminded that they, too, are worthy of the next level.

If there's a lesson in my reflection, it's this: *You don't have to have it all figured out to walk on purpose. You just have to be willing to look at yourself honestly, extend grace, and keep going.* The woman I see in the mirror today is evidence that you can lead, love, break, rebuild, and still rise.

THE JOURNEY

When I look in the mirror, I see a woman shaped by faith, resilience, and an unwavering commitment to purpose. I see a mother whose love knows no bounds—a woman who balances the weight of leadership, motherhood, and community advocacy with grace even when the road feels heavy. I see a servant leader who refuses to settle for mediocrity, driven by a calling to build wealth not just for herself but for those around her.

I see a romantic who, despite the heartaches she has grown through, still believes in love and loves deeply. I see a healing and beautiful heart full of hope, no longer defeated.

I see a warrior who has faced challenges head-on, carrying the wisdom of past struggles and the hope of a brighter future. I see a dreamer who envisions freedom—freedom to travel, create impact, and live in financial abundance without sacrificing precious moments with my son.

I see a Dominican queen who no longer believes that happiness comes from waiting for a Prince Charming. I see a woman who has learned to love herself as an imperfect masterpiece—beautifully flawed, resilient, compassionate, empathetic, graceful, complex, and joyful. I see the truth deep within my soul: My life is worth living, and I am fully capable of creating my own happiness.

I see a daughter of God, grounded in faith and fueled by love. I see a woman who refuses to be defined by her circumstances and instead chooses to write her own story—one of triumph, transformation, and purpose.

When I look in the mirror, I see the embodiment of perseverance, courage, and the audacity to dream big, knowing that I am worthy of every blessing on the horizon.

If there's a lesson in my reflection, it's this: *True strength is not found in perfection but in the ability to embrace every part of myself—my flaws, my struggles, my victories.* True strength is about showing up for myself, even when the journey feels overwhelming, and trusting that each step forward, no matter how small, is part of my greater purpose. It's about choosing to love myself fiercely, unapologetically, and recognizing that my worth isn't determined by others but by the power within me. *I am the author of my own story, and I hold the pen to shape my future.*

REPROGRAMMING YOUR LIFE

How do you reset your life when you've hit a wall? When your soul feels out of sync with your surroundings, and the person staring back at you in the mirror doesn't quite feel like you? The answer lies in conscious reprogramming—starting with small, sacred actions that bring you back into alignment with who you're becoming.

What if the mirror became less about judgment and more about *vision*?

Start seeing yourself through the lens of *possibility*. Visualize the version of you that honors your boundaries, lives in alignment with your purpose, and walks in your truth. Name that version. Write to her. Speak to her. Begin showing up every day as if you *are* already her—because you are. You don't become someone else. You return to the fullest expression of who you already are.

Every decision, every affirmation, every act of self-respect brings you closer to your true self.

First, you must reclaim your identity. Your identity is not who the world says you are; it's about who *you* decide to be. A simple yet powerful exercise to begin this work is to write the statement "I AM ____" five times, filling in the blanks with declarations that reflect your highest self. For example:

- I AM powerful.
- I AM worthy.
- I AM abundant.

THE JOURNEY

- I AM loved.
- I AM enough.

These aren't just affirmations; they're declarations. Each time you repeat them, you're planting seeds of truth and pulling up the weeds of old, limiting beliefs. You are rewiring your internal narrative and reminding yourself of the power you've always had, even when the world tried to convince you otherwise.

Transformation doesn't happen overnight. It happens in the quiet, daily decisions you make to show up differently. This is where rituals become your allies, such as meditation, prayer, journaling, crystal work, breathwork, or simply starting your morning with intention. These practices create the energetic space for your internal shift to take root and *reaffirm* the life you're building.

To reset is to pause. To realign is to listen. To reaffirm is to choose yourself again and again.

This process is not about becoming someone new but returning to the truth of who you've always been. Eventually, you'll realize that you are not only looking *into* the mirror—you *are* the mirror. You reflect the energy you carry. The way you treat yourself is the way you allow others to treat you. The love you withhold from yourself becomes the love you struggle to accept from others.

So ask yourself again: "Who do I see in the mirror?" If the answer isn't clear yet, that's okay. Keep showing up. Keep asking. Keep becoming. Every time you dare to look with courage and clarity, you get one step closer to the version of yourself you were always meant to embrace.

———————————— ————————————

After my divorce, I found myself at a crossroads, standing on the other side of a life I thought would last forever. In the wake of that chapter closing, I was forced to confront a version of myself that

Who Do You See in the Mirror?

felt broken, lost, and unsure of who I was outside of my marriage. I realized that rebuilding wasn't just about moving on from the past; it was about reclaiming myself, my dreams, and my identity. The journey to reset, realign, and reaffirm who I was and who I wanted to be was nothing short of transformative.

    The first step was a reset, a clean slate. I had to let go of everything I thought I knew about who I was in the context of a relationship. My worth had been entangled in being someone's partner, and when that role was no longer part of my life, I had to rediscover what made me whole on my own. This wasn't easy, especially with the feelings of failure and loss that often accompany divorce. But I realized that in order to move forward, I had to shed the weight of shame and guilt that clung to me and give myself permission to grieve. I grieved not only the end of my marriage, but the end of the dreams and expectations I had wrapped up in the identity of marriage. I believed getting married was my happy ending, or at least I had convinced myself of this story. When my biggest fear came to life and the marriage dissolved, I felt that I had been abandoned and discarded. To be honest, I wanted to die. The reset I did was about acknowledging my pain and choosing to heal from it rather than letting it define me. My faith, my family, and few close friends became my oxygen.

    Next came realignment. I had to realign my vision of what I wanted my future to look like. I had to reflect and acknowledge that I was not perfect. I had chosen the relationship/marriage; no one forced me into it. At this point, I had to surrender the dream of becoming a mother and leave it to God. God kept whispering in my heart that one day I would become a mother. Yet to me, this divorce was a loud message that I should give up on that promise because I could not envision having a family with anyone else. This was a hard process. I wish I could say it wasn't.

    My realignment was not about replacing the life I lost but about creating a new, improved version of my reality. I took time to reflect on my core values and goals—things I had put aside in the chaos of the relationship. I rediscovered my passion for personal growth, my love for travel, and the importance of my family and community. I realigned my priorities around my purpose: to build a life that was meaningful, fulfilling, and true to who I was becoming. I learned to let go of the expectations that society had placed on me about being married by age thirty and having a child by age thirty-five and instead create a new vision that reflected my true essence.

As I realigned, I also had to reaffirm my belief in love, not just as a romantic ideal but as an inherent part of who I was. I had to reaffirm my worth, my ability to love deeply, and my capacity to be loved. This reaffirmation wasn't about seeking validation from others; it was about giving it to myself. I chose to believe that I was worthy of the love I had dreamed of, even if the path to finding it looked different than what I had originally envisioned. I reaffirmed that I deserved to experience joy, peace, and fulfillment, regardless of the past. And even if I didn't get the opportunity to birth a child of my own, I could always adopt, foster, and be a great tia (aunt)! Learning to love myself again and knowing that I could stand on my own two feet, stronger than before, was a critical part of my healing.

Through this process of reprogramming my life, I also learned to embrace the journey of healing as a lifelong commitment. It wasn't about an instant fix or a quick turnaround but about small, intentional steps each day. There were moments when I doubted myself, when the weight of the past felt too heavy to bear, and tears would fall like a waterfall out of nowhere. But with every setback, I learned something valuable about myself. I developed resilience, perseverance, and a deeper understanding of who I was becoming. Healing didn't happen in one moment; it was a daily decision to continue moving forward, to continue showing up for myself, and to trust that my journey was leading me exactly where I was meant to go.

Now, looking back on my healing journey, I realize that the rebuilding process was not just about recovering from a divorce. It was about rediscovering who I was at my core, realigning my life with my true purpose, and reaffirming my worth. The journey was messy, sometimes painful, and often uncertain, but it was also empowering. Learning to forgive my former partner and myself and give ourselves grace and acknowledge this was our fate helps me feel gratitude for what we had. I am no longer angry or resentful. I have thanked that part of my life and those who were in it and now feel peace and confirmation that "everything worked out for my own good." Why? Because without that experience, I would not be this version of me. And, my God, I love who I am today!

Through it all, I learned that I am more than the circumstances I face. I am a woman capable of rewriting my own story, of reclaiming my happiness, and of building a life that is uniquely mine. By surrendering all that was, I was able to create what I prayed for over twenty years: to become a mother. Today, I am a grateful mother of a beautiful boy, and every time I see his smile, I know the journey to this moment was worth it. This process of reprogramming my life (resetting, realigning, and reaffirming) has shaped me into the person I am today, a woman who is not only healed but empowered and ready for whatever comes next.

ANCHORING YOUR IDENTITY MORNING AND EVENING ROUTINES

As we began to uncover who we truly were, we realized that identity isn't something you just discover—it's something you practice. The way we start and end each day plays a powerful role in shaping how we see ourselves and how we show up in the world. It became clear that consistency, not perfection, was key to grounding our growth. That's when we began creating intentional morning and evening

THE JOURNEY

routines that helped reinforce our values, clarity, and sense of purpose. Because the truth is, when you intentionally pour into yourself at the beginning and end of each day, you begin to rewrite the narrative of who you are and step boldly into who you're becoming. Here's a glimpse into what that looks like for each of us.

In a world that constantly pulls at your energy, *your routine becomes your anchor.* It's the place you return to when everything else feels like it's shifting. It's your steady ground, your private shoreline, where the noise fades and clarity begin.

As a nonprofit leader, entrepreneur, mother, elected official, and author, I've learned—often through burnout and overwhelm—that I cannot serve from an empty vessel. I cannot lead with intention if I haven't first made space to connect with myself. My routines are not rigid schedules; they are rituals of remembrance. They remind me of who I am before the world tries to tell me who to be.

Why Routines Matter

Routines aren't about checking off boxes or living by a strict schedule. They're about intentional connection—about building habits that ground you, restore you, and *center you in your truth.* Before you answer to anyone else's needs, you must first answer to your soul's needs. When you build routines rooted in identity (not productivity), you begin each day from a place of peace instead of panic. You end each night in reflection, not regret. That's the power of anchoring yourself through rhythm.

Think of the morning as a river's first ripple. It sets the tone for the day. The way you wake up impacts the way you show up. Instead of grabbing your phone and diving headfirst into chaos, try stepping into your day slowly and with *intention.*

My morning anchor points often include the following:

- *Stillness or prayer*: Before the noise begins, I sit in silence or talk with God. I ask for clarity, protection, and guidance.
- Movement: Whether it's stretching, walking, or a light workout, I move my body to awaken it with gratitude.
- *Affirmations and journaling*: I speak truth into my reflection and write down the intentions I want to carry with me.
- *Water*: Drinking water reminds me that replenishment is essential physically, mentally, and spiritually.

Your morning doesn't have to look like mine. It just has to feel *authentic* to you. The goal is to root yourself before the winds of the day try to uproot you.

The Evening Flow: Reflection and Release

Evening routines are equally sacred. In addition to preparing for you for rest, they *clear out what no longer belongs* so you don't carry the weight of the day into tomorrow. In the evening, I reflect. I ask myself: "Did I show up today? Did I lead with intention? Did I honor my values?" Even if I missed the mark, I give myself credit for every promise I kept to myself, big or small. I celebrate the quiet wins: the deep breaths, the boundaries held, the moments I chose grace over reaction.

Evening rituals are about *completion* and *compassion*. It's where I release the day, honor my effort, and reset for tomorrow without guilt. This practice has taught me the power of consistency—not in doing everything right, but in continuing to return to myself no matter what the day held. And on the hard days, when everything feels like too much, I lean into these routines like lifelines. Because they are. They remind me that who I am becoming is shaped in these quiet, repeated moments of intention. This is how we build self-trust. This is how we embody the identities we affirm.

THE JOURNEY

My evening flow might include the following activities:

- *Releasing the day*: A brain dump, a few journal lines, or even a moment of prayer to release what's on my heart.
- *Gratitude practice*: I take note of what I'm thankful for, even if the day felt hard.
- *Technology boundaries*: I create a buffer between my mind and the digital world so I can actually hear myself think.
- *Intentional winding down*: I read book, listen to soft music, or take deep breaths. Something that signals, "You did enough. Now, rest."

When I honor my evenings, I give myself permission to close the chapter on the day and trust that I don't need to carry everything overnight. Like water, I allow to flow what needs to flow, and what needs to settle, to settle.

Let me be clear: There are days my routines don't happen. There are mornings when I oversleep or nights when I fall asleep mid-prayer. But that doesn't make me less committed. Grace is a part of the practice. The power is not in the performance; it's in the *return*. Each time I choose to return to my rhythm, I'm choosing myself. I'm choosing peace over pressure, intention over impulse, and identity over chaos.

- How are you anchoring yourself in your truth?
- What rhythms can you build to remind you of your purpose?
- How can you make space for your soul before anyone else's demands enter the room?

Water flows, reflects, renews. And so do we. Your routine is not just a schedule. It's a sacred act of self-honoring.

Who Do You See in the Mirror?

In the morning before texts, meetings, and demands begin, I carve out time for me. Some days that looks like lighting a candle, breathing deeply, repeating my "I AM" affirmations of abundance, gratitude, and inspirational action, or journaling a few lines about my intentions for the day. Other mornings it's praying, sipping coffee or tea in silence, reading an inspiring book, or playing worship music that grounds me. What matters most is that I start with stillness—not striving. That space reminds me that I am not just a title or a to-do list. I am a woman with vision, with divine purpose, with power. I also take the time to remind myself that everything, including this moment, is working for my good! My routine becomes a declaration: "This day will not define me. I will define it."

ASSUMING YOUR TRUE IDENTITY

As we leaned deeper into the journey of self-discovery, we realized that uncovering your identity is only the beginning. The real transformation happens when you *assume* that identity—when you begin to walk, speak, and show up as the person you were always meant to be. It takes courage to release the versions of yourself shaped by fear, survival, or outside expectations. In the pages that follow, we each share what it looked like to step into our truth and embrace the fullness of our becoming.

Who you *believe* you are shapes how you show up in every space you enter—whether it's a boardroom, a community meeting, your child's school event, or a quiet moment at home. For a long time, I was showing up for the world while silently shrinking in the mirror. I knew how to put on the brave face, deliver the speech,

THE JOURNEY

lead the room, and advocate for others. But deep down, there were moments I questioned whether I was *really* enough.

And here's what I've learned: If your inner voice is whispering lies (*You're not ready. You're not worthy. You're not her.*), then you'll unknowingly start living that story. You'll accept less, dim your light, and second-guess your power. Not because you lack ability, but because your belief hasn't caught up to your calling.

But when you *assume* your true identity—the one rooted in divine design, personal truth, and lived resilience—you walk differently. You lead differently. You mother differently. You write, create, and love differently. You no longer wait for external validation because you've given yourself internal permission to take up space.

Assuming your true identity isn't about pretending to be someone else. It's about shedding the layers that life, trauma, or society placed on you and stepping fully into the woman you *already* are. The woman who has overcome public storms and private battles. The woman who's been stretched thin but never broke. The woman who didn't fold when it would've been easier to walk away. That woman is you. That woman is me.

As I've evolved (as a leader of a nonprofit, an elected official, a mother, and an author), I've realized that becoming her was never about finding something new. It was about *remembering* who I've always been. Living in alignment with your true identity changes your energy. You begin to treat the promises you make to yourself as sacred. Whether it's waking up early to write your vision, going for a walk to clear your mind, speaking up in a meeting, or simply resting because your body needed it, you must honor yourself. And each time you keep a promise, you deepen the trust between who you are and who you're becoming.

This is how you reclaim yourself. This is how you reset and reprogram your life. This is how you *show up* for others and for you yourself. And here's the secret: The world will always respond to how you see yourself. See yourself clearly. Boldly. Lovingly. Powerfully. Because *she*—the woman you're stepping into—is not waiting to be discovered. She is waiting to be claimed.

Remembering my true identity did not happen overnight. It was a journey that challenged me to dig deep and confront the woman I had become versus the woman I wanted to be. After my divorce, I found myself questioning my worth, my purpose, and my sense of self. I realized that for far too long, I had been living according to other people's expectations. I was showing up as the version of myself that I thought would make others happy or proud. But when the dust settled, I knew that I needed to rediscover who I truly was and reclaim my identity on my own terms.

The first step was giving myself permission to let go of the labels and roles that had confined me. No longer was I just someone's wife, someone's stepmother, someone's employee, or someone's problem-solver. I was a woman with dreams, passions, and a story worth telling. I embraced my cultural heritage with pride, reclaiming the strength and fire within me as a Dominican queen. I learned to speak kindly to myself, showing grace for past mistakes and compassion for the woman I was becoming. I gave myself room to heal, to forgive, and to rebuild—one step at a time.

Stepping into my true identity meant embracing my complexity and seeing myself as more than just the sum of my experiences. I became intentional about surrounding myself with people who uplifted me and poured into my growth. I stopped playing small and chose to live boldly, owning my story and walking in purpose. I understood that being authentic wasn't just about showing the strong and confident parts of me; it was also about being honest with my struggles and celebrating my growth. Living as my authentic self is a lifelong journey. Now, I stand firm in my identity—not as a reflection of others' expectations but as a woman who knows her worth and lives with unshakable purpose.

KEEPING YOUR PROMISES: RECLAIMING YOUR POWER

There's a quiet power in keeping your promises—not the ones you make to the world, but the ones you whisper to yourself in moments of clarity, conviction, or even quiet desperation. These promises are sacred. They're often made in the stillness of early mornings, in tearful prayers whispered through exhaustion, or in the silence of late nights when no one is watching. These are the moments where the most honest version of you speaks. Where you say:

- "I'm going to stop settling."
- "I deserve better."
- "I won't abandon myself again."
- "I will create space for my healing."

And yet, these are also the promises that are easiest to break because no one else is there to hold you accountable. There's no applause when you say no to what doesn't serve you. There's no audience when you decide to start over again. But that's the beauty of it. The power of these promises lies in the fact that *they are between you and you.*

When you start keeping these promises, something shifts. You begin to rebuild a bridge to your inner self—the part of you that has always believed in your potential, even when the outer world didn't reflect it. Every time you keep a promise to yourself, you are doing more than completing a task. You are proving that you are worthy of your own word. You are telling yourself, "I can trust you now." And that is where your true power lives—not in performance or perfection, but in self-trust.

Self-trust is the foundation of confidence. It's what fuels consistency. And it's what sustains you when no one else understands the journey you're on. Keeping your promises might look like:

- Choosing rest over burnout.
- Saying no when it's easier to say yes.
- Making time for your goals, even if it's just fifteen minutes a day.
- Removing yourself from spaces that make you shrink.
- Showing up for the version of you you've been praying to become.

These aren't always big, flashy moves. Sometimes the most powerful promises are the smallest ones—the decision to drink more water, to speak to yourself with kindness, to return to your routine after falling off for a few days. Small, repeated acts of self-loyalty are what transform lives.

Breaking those promises chips away at your power little by little. But the moment you decide to stop abandoning yourself, to stop giving others the best of you while giving yourself the leftovers is the moment you reclaim your power. And when you reclaim your power, you move differently. You speak with more clarity. You love with more freedom. You lead with more authenticity. You live with more alignment. Because now, you're no longer performing. You're walking in truth. You're walking in trust.

So today, ask yourself: "What promises have I made to myself that are still waiting to be honored? What part of me am I ready to reclaim by following through?" Start there. Keep one promise. Then another. And watch how the mirror begins to reflect not just who you are but who you've always had the power to become.

THE JOURNEY

I've made promises to myself in the middle of breaking points—after leaving meetings where I felt unseen, after crying behind closed doors because leadership felt heavy, after waking up from nights where sleep didn't come easy because my mind wouldn't stop replaying everything I didn't get to finish. I've made promises during doctor visits, during transitions, during the juggle of motherhood and mission-driven work. I've told myself, "You will not quit on you." And though I haven't always gotten it perfect, I've learned this: Every time I honored a promise to myself, no matter how small, I reclaimed a little more of my power.

Keeping your promises is sacred work. It's a sign that you respect yourself enough to follow through even when no one is watching. It is self-love in action. It is looking in the mirror and saying, "I got you" and meaning it. The more you do it, the more you begin to see yourself differently. You stop waiting for others to validate your worth or your work because you've already decided who you are.

- When I kept the promise to protect my peace, I walked away from spaces that no longer served me.
- When I kept the promise to rest, I learned that I didn't have to earn my right to slow down.
- When I kept the promise to show up fully in my work, even in the face of adversity, I remembered that I don't just have a seat at the table; I *am* the table.

That kind of consistency builds trust with *yourself.* And that self-trust becomes your foundation. It shows up in your confidence. In your posture. In your no. In your yes. In your ability to take up space unapologetically.

Who Do You See in the Mirror?

There was a time when keeping promises felt like second nature to me—promises to others, that is. I prided myself on being dependable, always showing up and going the extra mile. But somewhere along the way, I lost sight of keeping promises to myself. I poured so much energy into being everything for everyone that I forgot to honor my own needs, desires, and commitments. Procrastination became my escape, a way to cope with the overwhelming weight of expectations—both from others and from myself. I didn't realize that my tendency to overcommit and overdeliver was quietly burning me out. It wasn't that I loved breaking promises; it was that I was spreading myself too thin, trying to be the perfect version of me in everyone else's story.

The shift came when I had my son, Jireh. He was my answered prayer, my miracle, and I knew I couldn't continue living in that chaotic way. I wanted to be present with him, to create memories and nurture the bond between us. I had to make a choice: keep running myself ragged, or slow down and choose quality time with my son over everything else. I decided that being his mom meant showing up fully—not just physically but emotionally and mentally as well. So I pulled back from events, said no more often, and embraced a quieter, more intentional life. It wasn't easy. Some people still don't know I have a child! But I have chosen to protect my peace and prioritize my purpose as his mother, and that has made all the difference.

Today, I'm working daily to take inspired actions that align with my truth. I've come to understand that reclaiming my power means setting boundaries and being honest about what I can and cannot do. I no longer make promises out of guilt or obligation; instead, I commit to what aligns with my calling and purpose. I'm learning to let go of things that no longer serve me, shedding the need to please everyone. Keeping my promises (especially to myself) has become an act of self-respect and self-love. No matter how imperfect the journey, I choose to honor my word, not just to others but to the woman I am becoming.

SHOWING UP AUTHENTICALLY

How we show up in the world is often a mirror of how we feel about ourselves. It's not just about what we wear or say—it's the energy we bring into every room, the way we carry our story, and whether or not we allow ourselves to be seen *fully*.

If you've been showing up halfway, giving less than your best, or living on autopilot, trying to make it through the day, then I invite you to pause. Not to criticize yourself, but to check in with compassion and curiosity. Ask yourself: "What story am I believing about who I am?" "Is this belief rooted in truth or in a wound I haven't yet addressed?"

Sometimes we show up halfway because we're protecting ourselves from more disappointment. Other times it's because we've internalized a lie that says we're not enough, or that our worth is directly tied to how much we can produce or give. We shrink, we silence ourselves, and begin to mistake survival for authenticity. But here's the truth: Authenticity requires self-acceptance. You can't show up as your whole self if you don't *know* or *honor* your whole self.

As parents, there are days we give everything we have to our children—the last bite, the last ounce of patience, the last quiet moment of the day. We love deeply and serve sacrificially. But somewhere in that giving, it's easy to forget the sound of your own voice. You start to respond to names like "Mom" or "babe" or "boss," but when asked what *you* need, the question feels foreign.

As nonprofit leaders or community servants, there are seasons where you live in constant "go mode." You're fixing, planning, advocating, supporting. You become a solution machine. You carry people's stories, navigate crises, and bear witness to

Who Do You See in the Mirror?

suffering—often without fully acknowledging your own exhaustion. And if you're not careful, your identity starts to blur into your title, your mission, your impact. But titles are not your truth. Roles are not your identity. You were *someone* before the world asked you to serve. And you are still someone even when you're tired.

At work, I've had moments where the pressure to "perform" threatened to dim my authenticity. But even in those moments, I've had to remind myself: *You don't have to be perfect to be powerful. You just have to be present.*

Showing up authentically means no longer shrinking to fit into spaces you've outgrown. It means saying yes to alignment and no to self-abandonment. It means breaking up with old patterns, not because you've got it all figured out, but because you finally believe you deserve more.

Authenticity is not just a buzzword; it's a daily decision. A conscious choice to stop filtering yourself to make others more comfortable. It's the radical act of showing up as your whole self, even when it's inconvenient, misunderstood, or vulnerable.

For me, authenticity has been a lifelong lesson. I've spent years learning how to silence the noise and tune into *me*—the woman behind the titles, the deadlines, the expectations, and the appearances. And let me be honest, it's not always easy. As a nonprofit leader, I've felt the pressure to always have the answers, to constantly pour into others while sometimes running on empty myself. As an elected official, I've sat in rooms where I knew my presence was political before I ever opened my mouth—and still had to show up with grace, strength, and conviction. And as a mother, there have been countless moments where I wanted to be everything for everyone, all while learning how to finally be something for *myself.*

But here's what I know now: Showing up authentically doesn't mean you always feel strong. It means you choose honesty over performance. It means honoring your no with the same integrity you give to your yes. It means letting people experience the real you—not the curated version you think they'll accept.

Authenticity isn't about being loud. It's not about proving anything. It's about alignment. It's when your internal world matches the way you move externally. When your values, your voice, and your vision all sit in harmony, even when life feels messy. Some days showing up authentically might mean saying, "I don't have it all together today, but I'm still here." Other days it means standing tall, owning your brilliance, and refusing to shrink, even when your presence rattles the room.

Authenticity, no doubt, comes with risks. You might lose people. You might outgrow rooms. You might trigger discomfort in others who haven't yet given themselves permission to be real. But the reward? It's freedom. It's peace. It's walking through life without wondering if people love the mask or *you*.

When you show up authentically, you give others permission to do the same. You become a mirror, a model, and a movement all at once. And that's what the world needs: *not more perfection, but more truth*. More women rooted in who they are, refusing to apologize for it.

Take a moment to question your authenticity:

- Am I still performing?
- Am I still shape-shifting to fit the room?
- Am I still telling myself that the real me isn't enough?

Get ready to show up fully, flaws and all, and trust that *she*—the woman within you—is exactly who the world needs. Authenticity is your superpower. Use it. Own it. Walk in it unapologetically.

THE COST OF PERFORMING AND THE FREEDOM IN RETURNING

Authenticity doesn't require perfection. It simply asks for *presence*. It asks you to stop performing for approval or protection and to begin showing up from a place of self-trust. Authenticity says:

- "I don't need to pretend to be okay when I'm not."
- "I can be powerful and vulnerable in the same breath."
- "I'm allowed to evolve, even if that confuses the people who knew the former version of me."

There is such freedom in returning to yourself—not the curated version of you, but the *real* you. The one who has fears but also faith. The one who is growing, healing, reclaiming. The one who sometimes stumbles but always gets back up. Showing up authentically is not just for you; it gives others permission to do the same. When you model what it looks like to live from a place of truth, you shift the atmosphere around you. You become a mirror for others to see that it's okay to be real, raw, and *in progress*.

If you're struggling to show up authentically, start small. Return to the things that remind you of who you are outside of your responsibilities.

- What music makes you feel alive?
- What practices help you feel grounded?
- When's the last time you did something simply because *you* wanted to?

Create space for joy, curiosity, and quiet. Those moments help you reconnect with your spirit. And the more connected you are to your truth, the more confident and courageous you become in how you show up. To show up authentically is a daily choice. A choice to stop shrinking. A choice to lead with both heart and

THE JOURNEY

truth. A choice to stop abandoning yourself in the name of busyness or belonging.

Take a breath. Look in the mirror. Ask yourself, "What version of me do I need to show up as today?" Then move from that place with grace, honesty, and power.

Authenticity isn't a one-time decision. It is a daily devotion to being real. The more you return to yourself, the more powerful, magnetic, and grounded you become. You don't owe anyone a version of you that's filtered through fear. You owe yourself the freedom of being *fully you.*

♦ Christina
🦋 Maylin

PAUSE, REFLECT, AND REACT

Authenticity Audit

Take a moment and find a quiet space. Breathe deeply. This is your time to check in with *you*. Grab your journal, your favorite pen, and give yourself permission to be honest. You don't have to have it all figured out. This is about noticing, not judging. Let's begin:

1. **Who am I when no one is watching?**
   » When I strip away the titles, roles, and expectations, who am I at my core?
   » What do I truly enjoy, value, or believe in that I don't always express openly?
2. **Where am I still performing?**
   » Are there spaces where I feel the need to "play the part" or hide parts of who I am?
   » What am I afraid might happen if I showed up fully in those spaces?
3. **What stories am I still believing that keep me small?**
   » Write down any narratives that might still be playing in the background: "I'm not ready." "I don't want to make others uncomfortable." "I have to be perfect."
   » Now challenge those beliefs. Are they true, or are they simply habits?
4. **When was the last time I felt fully myself?**
   » Think of a moment (recent or distant) when you felt fully YOU.
   » What were you doing? Who were you with?
   » What would it look like to bring more of that energy into your everyday life?
5. **What does my authentic self need right now?**

- » Do you need rest? Permission? A boundary? A conversation? A deep breath?
- » Write a love note or affirmation to your most authentic self. (Example: "Dear Me, I give you full permission to speak freely, take up space, and be seen without apology. I've got you.")

6. **What is one way I can show up more authentically this week?**
   - » Think simple but intentional: saying no when you mean it, sharing your honest opinion in a meeting, wearing what makes you feel powerful, or carving out time for what fills your cup.
   - » Choose one authentic action and commit to it.

CHAPTER 9

The Responsibility of Being Great

To whom much is given, much is required.
—LUKE 12:48

Greatness begins where comfort ends.
—ROBIN SHARMA

GREATNESS SOUNDS GLAMOROUS—UNTIL you're the one called to carry it. We talk a lot about purpose, ambition, and elevation, but rarely do we talk about the cost. The truth is, stepping into your calling will stretch you, test you, and require more from you than you ever thought possible. It will pull you away from comfort. It will ask you to sacrifice, to confront your own fears, to lead even when you're exhausted. It's not just about reaching the mountaintop—it's about who you have to become to *stay* there.

THE JOURNEY

The responsibility of being great is not for the faint of heart. Because when much is given, *much is required*. That's not just a nice quote; it's a reality that will meet you in every room you step into, every decision you make, and every moment when no one is watching but your integrity is on the line. Greatness is heavy. It's inconvenient. It often demands that you go first, break the cycle, take the risk, speak the truth, stand alone. But here's the thing: It's also a *privilege*. To be chosen. To be called. To carry vision. To impact lives.

If you are meant for greatness, *simplicity is not an option*. You weren't built for average. You weren't created to blend in. Your journey will look different because your assignment *is* different. And that's okay. This chapter is about owning that weight, not resenting it. It's about rising to the challenge of your calling without shrinking from the responsibility it carries. Because being great isn't just about *doing* great things; it's about becoming someone who can be trusted with greatness.

Let's go there.

When I first heard the words "Your calling is going to crush you," I felt them settle in my bones. Not as a threat but as a truth I could no longer ignore. Those words didn't frighten me. Instead, they stopped me. They forced me to pause. To breathe. To reckon with the magnitude of what I was stepping into.

Because the truth is, greatness always comes at a cost.

What no one tells you when you say yes to the call is that you're also saying yes to the weight. Yes to being misunderstood. Yes to working when others rest. Yes to navigating lonely rooms, carrying other people's hope while trying not to lose your own. Yes to impact and yes to invisible scars.

If you're not willing to carry the weight of what you're called

The Responsibility of Being Great

to do, you risk forfeiting the fullness of the assignment. Because purpose won't always feel like a passion; it will often feel like pressure. And pressure doesn't mean you're doing it wrong. It means you're being shaped into someone who can be trusted with more.

I've spent years walking out an assignment that came with no clear instructions, only conviction. Building a nonprofit rooted in equity and empowerment didn't come with a manual. It came with late nights, hard conversations, and learning how to lead without losing myself. Running for public office and choosing to be a voice in spaces that were never designed for people like me—spaces that often silence us or distort our narratives—taught me that visibility doesn't always come with validation.

And then there's the sacred role of motherhood. Raising children while I'm still learning how to raise myself in certain areas. Trying to model strength while still healing. Trying to teach them how to grow roots while I'm still planting mine. There's no off switch, no pause button, no perfect formula.

It's all intertwined—the leadership, the purpose, the public work, the private wrestling. None of it is simple. But that's the point. Greatness was never supposed to be easy. It was supposed to be *earned, embodied*, and carried with care.

Let's talk about what often gets left out of the conversation. The long days that turn into long nights with no time to rest, and the toll it takes on your body. The guilt of missing moments with family because you're pouring into the world. The silent prayers whispered in your car, your shower, or between emails, asking for peace in a life that often feels like it's moving too fast to catch your breath.

Greatness will stretch you. It will ask you to give more than you thought you had. And if you're not careful, it will convince you to give until there's nothing left. That's why boundaries matter. That's why rest is not a reward but a responsibility. That's why you must protect your peace with the same intensity that you protect your purpose. Because the world will always take as much as you're willing to give. But it's up to you to say, "I'm not going to sacrifice my well-being to prove my worth. I can be powerful and rested. Purposeful and human."

I often say I've never been bored since I met Christina! Once God connected us, my life became a journey of growth. And let me tell you, it hasn't been easy. Back in 2010, I had a simple vision for my life: Get married, stay married forever, have a family, work the same job until retirement, love God, and be kind to people. It seemed like a great plan in theory, a life marked by stability and faith. But then Christina came along, and everything changed.

Throughout our growing friendship, I discovered a burning desire to grow, to serve my community, and to support women in ways I didn't even have words for back then. I just knew I wanted to make an impact. When we started working together in service, it felt foreign—not just to me but to those who knew the old version of me. I had left the corporate world behind to dive into nonprofit work, and I've been here ever since. I became a powerhouse, a woman on fire for change. There was nothing I believed was impossible. Whether it cost me my savings, my paycheck, or my time, I made sure it happened. We both did! That relentless dedication to serve is what fueled our growth. We were willing to do whatever it took to make a difference.

As I stepped into my calling, I lost a lot: friendships, dreams, and parts of myself I thought were essential. Looking back, I realize they served a purpose at that point in my life, but they couldn't come with me into the next phase of the journey. I began to feel the responsibility of being great—a weight I didn't sign up for but that had been assigned to me. At the time, I didn't fully understand it, and it felt heavier than was probably necessary.

The Responsibility of Being Great

But through that pressure, I was shaped and strengthened, building resilience and wisdom I didn't know I needed. The biggest lesson in that season was realizing that God had chosen me, even when I didn't feel worthy or capable. I also learned that having the right friendship and business partner was essential to fulfilling my assignment. Now, over fifteen years later, it feels like time has flown by, yet we've built so much. We still haven't accomplished everything on our business plan, but we are deeply grateful for the journey and the opportunity to serve as we've been called to do.

Leadership is not something you chase; it's something that calls you. And when it calls, it rarely does so when you feel ready. It shows up in moments of discomfort, in whispers of conviction, in circumstances that demand courage. True leadership isn't about titles, attention, or validation. It's about responsibility, resilience, and the willingness to rise when others retreat. It's a sacred assignment that chooses you. And once it does, you can't unsee the need, the gap, the purpose you were born to fill. The calling to lead is less about being in control and more about being in position. Positioned to serve. Positioned to shift culture. Positioned to carry vision even when it feels heavy. And once you say yes to that calling, your life will never be the same.

THE CALLING TO LEAD

Leadership (*real* leadership) is not glamorous. It's not filtered through curated Instagram posts, panel discussions, or polished titles. It's not about applause after the speech or the compliments after the event. The calling to lead often begins in silence. In discomfort. In a quiet stirring that tells you: *There is more to do. And you've been chosen to help do it.*

Real leadership is lonely. It's messy. It's sacred. It's staring at the ceiling at two a.m. replaying decisions in your mind, wondering if you did the right thing, said too much or not enough, or let someone down in a way you can't fix. It's wiping your tears in the bathroom before showing up to lead a meeting that can't afford your breakdown. It's walking into the room with poise and presence even when you're still bleeding from battles no one else sees.

Leadership will stretch you. It will humble you. And if you let it, it will also transform you. People often see the outcome, not the process. They see the platform but not the preparation. They see the results but not the wrestle. Leadership requires four core elements:

- Making hard decisions that no one else wants to carry.
- Being the one who takes the blame when things go wrong, and often receiving no credit when things go right.
- Navigating criticism from people who've never had to sit in your seat.
- Knowing that you're not always going to be liked, and learning how to be okay with that.

It's carrying the weight of people's hopes while trying to hold on to your own humanity. And yet you keep showing up. Not because it's easy. Not because you always feel ready. But because the calling won't let you sit still. Because something in you knows that this is what you were built for, even when it's uncomfortable.

Leadership is the emotional toll no one talks about. Let's be honest. There are moments in leadership that will break your heart.

- Moments where you feel the pressure to be "on" all the time.
- Moments where your values are tested.
- Moments where you're expected to pour, even when your cup is empty.
- Moments where you wonder if the sacrifices are worth it.

You'll question yourself. You'll want to quit. You'll crave rest, freedom, *normalcy*. But leadership is not a job; it's a calling. And

The Responsibility of Being Great

a calling doesn't go away just because you're tired. It whispers, even in the dark. It tugs at your soul and says, *Not yet. There's still more.*

But hear this clearly: You don't have to lose yourself in the name of leadership. You don't have to burn out to prove that you care. You can lead with integrity and still protect your peace. You can be both powerful *and* tender.

Leadership isn't about being perfect—it's about being present. It's about being bold enough to go first, honest enough to admit when you're unsure, and wise enough to surround yourself with truth-tellers who remind you of your purpose when the path gets blurry.

You were never called to lead *like them*. You were called to lead *like you*.

> With your story.
> With your scars.
> With your values.
> With your voice.

And that voice? It doesn't have to be the loudest in the room to make an impact. It just has to be *anchored*.

So if you're in a season of leadership where it feels like no one sees the weight you're carrying, know this: Leadership is not about being above others. It's about being deeply rooted in service, in conviction, and in the responsibility of influence. You don't have to get it right all the time. You just have to keep showing up with heart. That's what makes you a leader.

I remember sitting alone in my car after a board meeting that had left me feeling emotionally drained. I had advocated for what

I knew was right, knowing full well it wouldn't be the popular decision. That night, I cried. Not because I doubted myself, but because I understood the weight of what I was carrying. That's what greatness does. It humbles you. It stretches you. It calls you to stand firm when everything around you is pushing back.

The calling to lead isn't just about being in charge; it's about being *anchored*. Anchored in your values. Anchored in your vision. Anchored in a belief that even when it hurts, even when you're tired, *this matters*. When you are called to lead, you aren't given a choice to play small or hide in comfort. The path to greatness requires ownership of that calling, even when it feels overwhelming.

YOU DON'T GET TO BE REGULAR

If you've been called to greatness, you've probably felt it in those moments when you wanted to just blend in, do less, say nothing. But something inside wouldn't let you. That's the burden. And the gift.

There have been seasons where we watched others coast (no pressure, no push), and we admit that we often envied their easy path. We've wanted to shrink, to say, "Maybe we're doing too much," and take the easier path. But then we remembered we weren't built for easy. We were built for impact. For disruption. For elevation. And so are you.

You don't get to be regular when you're called to shift systems, spark healing, and open doors for others. Simplicity may be comfortable, but greatness requires something more. It demands integrity when no one's watching, grit when you feel depleted, and vision when the path is still unclear.

Leadership is not about being in charge; it's about taking charge of your mindset, your actions, and the influence you wield. To be great, you must shift from a *fixed mindset*, where you believe your abilities are static, to a *growth mindset*, where

The Responsibility of Being Great

you believe your abilities can be developed with effort and perseverance. This is the foundation of greatness. You can't afford to ask, "Why can't I just be simple?" because simplicity isn't your destiny.

Here's what we've come to believe: Greatness is not just a burden. It is a privilege. You've been trusted with influence. Trusted with insight. Trusted with impact. And while it's exhausting at times, it's also sacred.

When young girls see us lead, we don't just represent a title, we represent possibility. When someone reads this book or hears us speak and says, "Because of you, I kept going," the crushing weight becomes light. When we lay our heads down at night, knowing we led with integrity even when it cost us, *that* is the reward.

So yes, your calling may feel like it's crushing you. But maybe that pressure isn't here to break you. Maybe it's here to mold you. Refine you. Remind you of who you are and what you were always meant to become. If you're feeling the weight right now, know this: You are carrying something *divine*. Something bigger than your comfort. Something tied to legacy, not likes. Purpose, not popularity.

As for us? We've learned not to run from the pressure but to rise with it. To embrace the tension between the crushing and the calling. Why? Because in that space, greatness is born. One of the most transformative things you can do on your journey toward greatness is change the quality of the questions you ask yourself. For years, we found ourselves sitting with the same questions, especially in moments of exhaustion, disappointment, or public pressure: "Why me? Why is this happening? Why does it always feel this hard?"

And while those questions were honest, they weren't helpful. We had to learn that questions are not just thoughts; they are *directions*. They guide your mind toward meaning. And if you're constantly asking questions rooted in defeat or fear, your thoughts will mirror that. But when you shift the question, you shift the entire conversation you're having with yourself.

Instead of asking, "Why is this happening to me?" we began asking:

- "What is this trying to teach me?"
- "Who am I becoming through this?"
- "How can I respond in a way that aligns with the woman I am becoming?"
- "What is the lesson and opportunity?"

These questions don't ignore the pain; they reframe it. They move you from victimhood to vision. From reacting to *responding*. And from surviving to evolving.

In our roles—whether advocating as an elected official, leading a nonprofit through uncertainty, or mothering while managing everything else—we've had to get really intentional about the internal dialogue we allow. Because the questions you ask shape your thoughts. Your thoughts shape your beliefs. And your beliefs shape every single action you take.

If you want to take ownership of your leadership, your purpose, and your impact, it starts with asking better questions.

- Questions that hold you accountable, not hostage.
- Questions that unlock growth, not guilt.
- Questions that open doors instead of reinforcing walls.

Leadership is not about having all the answers. It's about having the *right questions* that challenge you to rise even when the odds are stacked against you. The questions that push you to evolve when it would be easier to shrink.

The next time life feels heavy and the pressure starts to mount, take a deep breath and ask yourself: "What is the most empowering

The Responsibility of Being Great

question I can ask in this moment?" That one shift might not change your situation immediately, but it will change *you*—and that's where true leadership begins and resilience activates.

But what exactly is resilience? Is it something you're born with, or is it forged through experience?

For me, resilience has never felt like a single aha moment or a bolt of lightning from the sky. It's never been about one defining speech, one big win, or one triumphant comeback that made it all better. Resilience, for me, has shown up in the quiet, gritty, often invisible decisions I make every single day. It has lived in the moments when no one was watching. When I had every reason to quit, to stay silent, and to shrink but chose to rise anyway.

It's looked like continuing to serve my community after being publicly scrutinized and misrepresented, facing headlines and whispers that tried to distort my character. I've had to learn how to stand tall in the storm, not because it didn't shake me, but because the work was bigger than my feelings. Because my purpose didn't stop just because my confidence wavered.

Resilience has looked like leading a nonprofit with limited resources but unlimited passion, navigating budget gaps, staffing challenges, and endless to-do lists while still showing up with vision. Still showing up for the girls and women who were waiting for someone to believe in them. Still pushing forward when the systems weren't designed for people like us to win. We created our own tables. We became the door when none would open.

It has looked like crying in my car or in the shower—spaces where I could let it all out—only to wipe my face, straighten my posture, and walk into a boardroom with fire in my voice and strategy on my mind. Because I knew what was at stake. Because

I knew that every time I showed up, I wasn't just advocating for myself. I was standing in the gap for those who hadn't yet found their voice.

Resilience, to me, isn't loud. It's sacred. It's steady. It's the decision to keep becoming, especially when it hurts. It's the refusal to let the weight of life keep me from rising. Again and again. Not because I don't feel the pressure. But because I've learned how to move through it with grace, grit, and God.

That's resilience.

For me, resilience is the unwavering determination to rise above challenges, no matter how heavy the burden or how deep the wound. It's having a divorce via Zoom, allowing myself to cry once the hearing was over, then wiping away the tears and telling myself, "Even this moment is working out for my good." It's summoning the strength to mask the pain behind makeup and show up with an energy of gratitude and service. Why? Because I knew the calling was bigger than me, bigger than us.

In my role as a national director for an organization that breathes "children first" in the world of foster care, and as a co-founder of another nonprofit dedicated to empowering girls and women in my community, I channeled that pain into purpose. I poured my heart into creating programs that would go on to support thousands of children—not just in Central Ohio but across the United States, its territories, and even a few countries beyond.

Resilience is the ability to turn heartache into hope, to transform setbacks into stepping stones, and to keep moving forward when life tests your resolve. Resilience is honoring both my body and mind, knowing when to push forward and when to rest, because taking care of myself is essential to sustaining my strength and purpose. Rest is not weakness; it's an act of courage that prepares me to keep showing up with grace and determination. It's knowing that no matter how tough the journey gets, I will rise—stronger, wiser, and more determined to make a difference in the lives of those I'm called to serve.

THE TRUTH ABOUT RESILIENCE

Resilience is not about being unbothered or unbreakable. Let's set that myth aside right now. It's not about smiling through every storm or pretending nothing affects you. Real resilience is about being *stretched*—sometimes beyond what you think you can bear—and still choosing not to *snap*.

It's about bending under pressure without losing your shape. It's about the moments when life knocks the wind out of you, and somehow, you find the courage to inhale again. Not because it's easy, but because deep down, something in you knows your story doesn't end here.

Resilience is not a personality trait you're either born with or without. It's a skill, a spiritual muscle, that gets stronger every time you use it. And like any muscle, it's built through pressure, repetition, and recovery. That cultivation starts in your mind.

We've all lived through seasons where our minds gave up before our bodies ever did. When your heart still wanted to fight, but your thoughts whispered, *What's the point?* When the criticism got louder than the calling. When the weight of being "everything to everyone" made you question whether you were ever enough for yourself.

In those moments, a **fixed mindset** would've said:

- "This is too hard."
- "You're not built for this."
- "Sit this one out."

But a **growth mindset** said:

- "You've been through worse."
- "You are growing through this."
- "This is just another stretch on the climb."

The difference between breaking and becoming often lies in which voice you choose to believe.

BUILDING RESILIENCE, BRICK BY BRICK

Every time you move through adversity and choose perseverance over passivity, you strengthen your resilience muscle. You create an inner toughness—not a hardness that disconnects you from your emotions, but a softness rooted in self-compassion and purpose.

Yes, self-compassion matters. As a woman committed to so many—your children, your community, your vision—it's easy to fall into the trap of self-sacrifice. But we've learned (sometimes the hard way) that pushing through pain without ever acknowledging it doesn't make you strong; it makes you suffer in silence. Resilience is about giving yourself permission to pause, reflect, heal, and then rise stronger.

Because the responsibility of being great isn't about perfection. It's about *persistence*. It's about the willingness to get back up, to reset your posture, and to continue moving in the direction of your purpose no matter how many times you've been knocked off course.

Resilience is built in the moments no one sees. It's built when you get up early to realign your thoughts before the world demands your energy. It's built when you choose grace instead of guilt after a rough day in motherhood or leadership. It's built when you whisper to yourself, "Keep going," even when you don't feel like it.

THE PRICE AND PRIVILEGE OF GREATNESS

Greatness is both a weight and a reward. It asks everything of you and gives everything in return. Greatness is often romanticized. We admire the outcomes (success, recognition, influence), but rarely do we discuss what it actually *costs* to stand in your greatness. And make no mistake, there is a price.

To be called to greatness means you will walk a road that is anything but easy. You'll be asked to carry what others can't, to lead when others follow, to rise when quitting would be justified. You will be called to stretch beyond your comfort, to be disciplined when no one is watching, and to hold your standards even when you're tired, overlooked, or misunderstood.

Greatness will ask for your time. Your focus. Your consistency. Your peace. Sometimes even your health, your sleep, or your relationships—if you're not careful to protect them. It's not just about what you gain; it's about what you *surrender* to be able to carry what you're called to steward.

Sure, greatness includes the impact people see on the outside. More importantly, though, it's about the internal transformation that happens when you commit to evolving, again and again. Greatness isn't a destination you arrive at one day, dressed in accolades. It's a journey—a daily, often messy process of becoming. And that journey requires resilience, responsibility, and radical self-awareness.

Yes, this path is heavy. But it is also sacred. You were chosen for this life not because it's easy, but because you are *equipped*. Your lived experiences, your scars, your failures, and your fire are not detours. They are the very tools shaping your voice, your presence, and your power.

When the weight of your calling feels like too much, I want you to remember this: You were *never* built for average. You were *always* built for impact. And everything you need to fulfill your purpose already exists within you.

THE JOURNEY

The real question isn't, "Can you handle it?" but "Are you willing to take full responsibility for being great?" Your legacy doesn't begin when things get easy. It begins the moment you choose to keep going, even when it's hard.

⬩ Christina
🦋 Maylin

PAUSE, REFLECT, AND REACT

Writing Your Way Back to You

Use this space to slow down and sit with the truths in this chapter. Remember, growth doesn't happen in the rush; it happens in the *pause*. Let your answers flow honestly and without judgment. You're not writing for perfection. You're writing to reconnect with yourself.

What are you inspired to stop doing?

1. What limiting beliefs or lies about yourself are you ready to release?
2. What habits are keeping you in survival mode instead of alignment?
3. In what ways have you been shrinking, playing small, or silencing your truth?
4. What self-sabotaging behavior has been costing you peace, joy, or progress?
5. Who or what are you giving energy to that no longer reflects the person you're becoming?

What are you inspired to start doing today?

1. What is one promise you're ready to keep to yourself, starting today?
2. How can you intentionally show up more authentically this week?
3. What new boundary, routine, or practice can you implement to protect your peace and energy?
4. How can you lead or serve from a place of overflow rather than depletion?
5. What does the next version of you need from *you* in order to rise?

CHAPTER 10

The Journey Continues

*There is no end to the journey. There is
only the next chapter, the next sunrise,
the next version of who you're meant to become.*

—UNKNOWN

AS WE COME to the end of this book, it's important to remember that personal growth and leadership are lifelong pursuits, not finish lines. The transformation you've begun isn't defined by the turning of these final pages, but by the ongoing decisions you'll make, the habits you'll cultivate, and the courage you'll summon moving forward. You are still becoming. And becoming takes time.

Throughout this journey, you've revisited your reflection, rewritten your narrative, and realigned with your purpose. You've explored the power of your voice, the importance of boundaries, the necessity of community, and the resilience required to rise when life knocks you down. But even with all the progress you've made, this is not the end. It's an invitation to go deeper.

Growth is not a one-time event, and success is not a final stop. Each chapter in this book has been a stepping stone toward a more authentic, grounded, and purpose-driven version of yourself. The choices you've made, the relationships you've nurtured, the boundaries you've set, and the resilience you've cultivated are the building blocks for the future you are continuously creating.

So what now?

You keep going. You keep growing. You keep showing up for yourself, especially on the hard days.

The journey continues every time you recommit to your values. Every time you honor your voice. Every time you keep a promise to yourself. Let this time we have spent together be a reminder that there is no arrival, only evolution. You don't need to have it all figured out to move forward. You just need to be willing. Willing to keep asking the hard questions. Willing to keep learning. Willing to keep becoming.

This final chapter isn't an ending. It's a handoff to your future self. The one who's watching you from the mirror, cheering you on. She's already proud. She already knows how far you've come. And she's waiting patiently for you to meet her on the other side of every brave choice you make.

Think back to chapter 1: "My Current Self vs. My Future Self." The gap between who you are today and who you want to become is not a fixed distance. As you grow, evolve, and pursue your goals, the future self you envision will shift and expand. That's the beauty of the journey. There is always more to learn, more to strive for, and more room for improvement.

Self-growth is not about reaching a final form but about becoming a better version of yourself each day. Life will continue to throw new challenges your way, and with each challenge comes the opportunity to rise higher. You've planted seeds in chapter

The Journey Continues

3—seeds of change, discipline, and self-awareness. Those seeds will continue to grow as you water them with perseverance and intentional action.

Along this path, you will inevitably encounter obstacles. There will be days when you question whether you are on the right path or if the effort is worth it. But as we discussed in chapter 6: "A Single Bad Day Doesn't Define Your Whole Life," it's not the setbacks that matter but how you respond to them.

Resilience, a theme explored in chapter 9: "The Responsibility of Being Great," will be your guiding force. The ability to bounce back, to adapt, and to continue striving for greatness, even when things get tough, is what will sustain your growth. Understand that your journey won't always be smooth, but each hurdle is an opportunity to grow stronger and wiser.

One of the key pillars of continuous growth is lifelong learning. In a world that is always changing, your ability to learn, adapt, and reflect will determine how far you go. Think about the importance of "clearing the air" in chapter 2. Just as you had to confront past hurts, misunderstandings, or misconceptions to move forward, you must also clear the way for new knowledge and experiences. Stagnation occurs when we think we've learned everything we need to know. But true growth happens when you embrace a learner's mindset, always curious, always open to new perspectives.

Lifelong learning is about gaining knowledge and understanding from your daily experiences, from the people you meet, and from the moments that challenge you. It's about cultivating curiosity, constantly asking yourself, *"How can I grow from this? What new understanding can I gain?"* Each day provides an opportunity for reflection and refinement.

In chapter 8: "Who Do You See in the Mirror?" we explored the importance of understanding who you truly are. This awareness is critical as you continue on your journey. The more aligned you are with your true self and purpose, the easier it will be to navigate the complexities of life.

Your purpose will serve as your North Star, guiding you through the twists and turns of your journey. There will be times when the path ahead is unclear, but as long as you are committed to your purpose, you will find a way forward. Revisit the affirmations, the meditations, and the routines that help keep you grounded, as they will serve as powerful tools in moments of doubt.

One of the most empowering realizations is that you always have the power to choose. In chapter 4: "Can Your No Mean No?" we discussed the importance of setting boundaries. As you move forward in your journey, remember that your choices will continue to shape your future. Each decision, big or small, contributes to the trajectory of your life.

Will you choose to keep showing up for yourself even when you don't feel like it? Will you choose to say yes to opportunities that push you out of your comfort zone, knowing that growth lies just beyond the edge of discomfort? The responsibility of greatness, as we explored in chapter 9, demands that you take ownership of these choices.

Progress is not linear, but every step forward counts. In chapter 7: "A Pathway to Progress," we explored how to build a life that moves steadily toward your goals. This pathway is ongoing, with no final destination. Each achievement is simply a milestone on a much larger journey.

The key is to celebrate the small wins and to honor the progress you make, even when it feels incremental. Remember, the destination is not what defines you; it's the journey that shapes you. Continue to trust the process, and give yourself grace as you move forward.

Finally, remember the promise you made to yourself at the beginning of this book: the promise to become the best version of yourself. Keeping that promise will require dedication, persistence, and a willingness to embrace change. But it will also require self-compassion. You won't always get it right, but as long as you keep moving forward, you are honoring that commitment.

The journey continues, and with it comes the opportunity to grow into the person you are destined to be. It's not about arriving at a place of perfection—it's about showing up, day after day, as the person you want to be, knowing that every step you take brings you closer to your higher self.

Transformation is a process, not a destination. Each small action, every hard-won victory, and even the occasional stumble play a role in shaping your journey. Celebrate the moments when you feel aligned with your purpose, and learn from the moments when you feel off course. They all hold value in the grander picture of your life.

CULTIVATING YOUR VISION

To continue growing, you must cultivate your vision. Revisit your goals regularly and ask yourself:

- Am I staying true to my values?
- Am I prioritizing what truly matters?
- What adjustments can I make to stay on course?

The answers to these questions may evolve over time, just as you will. Be open to the shifts that life brings and trust that each change is an opportunity for deeper alignment with your authentic self.

Your journey is not just for you. The work you do to become your best self radiates outward, touching the lives of those around you. By honoring your promise to yourself, you become a source of inspiration and a guidepost for others seeking their own paths.

As you continue forward, think about the legacy you are building. What lessons, values, or inspiration do you want to leave behind? How can your journey uplift and empower others?

THE POWER OF NOW

As you reach this point in your journey, pause and take a breath. Let this be your reminder that the most powerful place you can ever be is right here in the present moment. The past has shaped you and the future will inspire you, but it is *now* that holds the key to your transformation.

You don't need permission, a perfect plan, or the "right" timing to begin again. You simply need to be present and awake to your life as it is, open to who you are becoming, and willing to take the next step forward. Every day offers a fresh invitation to return to yourself, to realign with your purpose, and to recommit to the promises you've made to your soul.

The beauty of now is that it doesn't ask for perfection; it simply asks for presence. In this moment, you can choose to show up with grace. You can decide to lead with courage. You can take one small action that nudges you closer to your truth. And that one act, repeated over time, becomes your path to growth.

There is deep freedom in learning to live here in the now. It's where healing begins, where clarity takes shape, and where peace finds its way into your heart. Let go of the regrets that try to keep you anchored to yesterday. Release the worry that tries to steal your joy about tomorrow. Neither of those moments belong to you anymore. But *this* one does.

Right now, you have everything you need to move forward. The strength, the wisdom, and the fire are already inside of you. You've already made it through things you once thought would break you. You've risen more times than you've fallen. And every lesson, every scar, every moment has brought you here for a reason.

Take a moment. Reflect. Honor how far you've come. Celebrate the version of yourself who refused to quit even when things felt heavy or unclear. You may not be exactly where you want to be yet, but you are walking in the right direction with purpose, with persistence, and with power.

The Journey Continues

WALKING FORWARD

As you close this chapter, know that every step forward matters. Progress isn't always flashy or dramatic; sometimes it is quiet, steady, and deeply personal. Growth often happens in the spaces where no one is watching. Where your resilience meets your reflection. Where your choices speak louder than your doubts. But every step you take with courage, kindness, and purpose moves you closer to the best version of yourself.

Even when the path feels uncertain, trust that the person you're becoming is already within you—waiting, ready, and fully capable. You don't need to have all the answers today. What matters most is that you keep showing up. Keep choosing growth over fear, alignment over approval, and purpose over pressure.

You are worth every moment of effort. Every ounce of dedication. Every sacred pause and bold decision it takes to walk this journey. Keep moving forward. The transformation is already happening right here, in this very moment. That's the power of now.

No one else in the world has walked the path you're about to embark on. Your journey is uniquely yours—shaped by your dreams, your scars, your hopes, and your healing. Every experience has prepared you. Every challenge has revealed something resilient in you.

This is your invitation to embrace who you are today while daring to step into who you are becoming. Trust your intuition. Honor your voice. Celebrate your growth, even when it's messy. Along the way, you'll uncover new strengths, rediscover forgotten dreams, and learn how to stand tall in your truth.

You'll lose some things (and some people) on the journey. But what you'll gain is far greater: a deeper knowing of self, a more anchored sense of purpose, and the unshakable belief that you were made for more.

The twists and turns become opportunities to evolve. Not into someone new, but into the truest version of who you've always been. Walk forward with courage. Move with intention. Speak with love. And live like the journey itself is the reward.

Because it is.

Your story isn't finished. In fact, it's just beginning.

And the next chapter? It's going to be extraordinary.

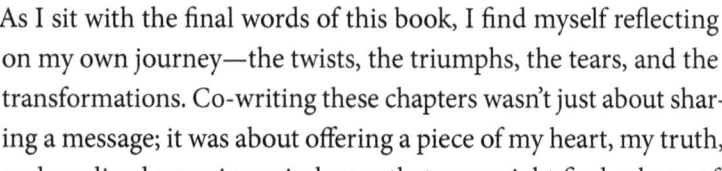

As I sit with the final words of this book, I find myself reflecting on my own journey—the twists, the triumphs, the tears, and the transformations. Co-writing these chapters wasn't just about sharing a message; it was about offering a piece of my heart, my truth, and my lived experience in hopes that you might find echoes of your own story within these pages.

The Journey: From Who You Are to Who You're Meant to Be is more than a title. It's a lived truth. One I've come to know intimately. Like you, I've questioned my worth, wrestled with fear, and stood at the edge of uncertainty, wondering if I had what it took to keep going. And like you, I've also discovered just how powerful it is to keep choosing myself—to keep rising, keep healing, and keep walking toward the version of me I know I'm meant to be.

This book is a reminder that you are not alone. You're not behind. You're not broken. You're becoming. Every chapter has been an invitation to reflect, to reimagine, and to reclaim the power that's always lived within you. And my hope is that as you close this book, you do so with more clarity, more confidence, and more compassion for yourself than you had when you began. You don't have to have it all figured out to be on the right path. You just have to be willing to take the next step. One choice at a time. One day at a time.

Thank you for allowing me to be part of your journey. I'm cheering for you—always. And I can't wait to see how boldly and how beautifully you continue to walk forward.

The Journey Continues

You made it to the last chapter. Congratulations! Your commitment is impressive, and getting to this part of the book wasn't easy. Just like you, Christina and I have been on a journey with this book for several years. Life kept happening, and we would pause, then keep going, and then pause again. Finally, Christina said, "The world needs our message. Let's finish what we started. It's time!"

It took me a while to sit down and do my edits here and there because, if you know Christina and me, you know we're visionaries. We plan things, we manifest things, and we've learned to recognize when it's time to birth an idea. This is that time. Yet I had my doubts. Who would read our book? Should I share or keep my life private? Then it hit me. Playing small was helping no one. I have a special gift, just like you do, placed within me by God to guide me in fulfilling my calling. Sometimes I've hidden from it because when I shine too brightly, it draws attention. And while I love people, I never wanted this to be about me. I want it to be about my assignment—about impacting every soul God intends me to reach through my voice.

With the conviction that this is bigger than me, knowing that even one person might need my message to take that next step, I built up the courage to write my part—my contribution. Christina, my accountability partner, gave me a deadline, and I knew I had until that date for the initial draft before the editor worked her magic. I prayed, made coffee, got up at 4:30 a.m., and started writing. The words poured out so fast I couldn't stop. Within twenty-four hours, I had given my heart to my final edits—and boom, here we are! I'm so grateful that fear and doubt didn't stop me from believing in the power of my voice, and I ask you to do the same.

What is that one thing God has called you to do? Write a book, launch a podcast, create that product, take that trip, or start that business? This is your confirmation that the time is now. Tomorrow is not promised. My mother's words still guide me to this

THE JOURNEY

day: "Do what you can today. Don't put off for tomorrow what you can do today!"

You have greatness within you, and the world needs your voice, your story, your vision. Don't wait for the perfect moment. Instead, create it. Step out with courage and let your light shine. You've got this, and now we've got your back!

Keep journeying. Keep becoming. And never forget: You are the author of what comes next.

⁂ Christina
🦋 Maylin

PAUSE, REFLECT, AND REACT

Your Journey Toolkit
Reflections & Affirmations for the Road Ahead

Before you close this book, take a moment to pause and check in with yourself. Growth is not about how quickly you move; it's about how deeply you stay connected to your purpose.

REFLECTION PROMPTS

Use these journal prompts to stay rooted in your journey and reignite your intentions as needed:

1. What part of myself am I most proud of today?
2. Which chapter or lesson from this book impacted me the most, and why?
3. Where in my life am I still playing small or hiding? What is it costing me?
4. What does my "next level" look like. What small action can I take this week to align with it?
5. How can I honor both who I've been and who I'm becoming?
6. What is one belief, relationship, or habit I need to release in order to grow?
7. What do I want to remember when things get hard or uncertain?

Tip: Revisit these prompts monthly or quarterly to check your alignment and celebrate your progress.

THE JOURNEY

AFFIRMATIONS TO ANCHOR YOUR BECOMING

Speak these words aloud or write them where you'll see them daily. Let them become your anchor when the waters of life get choppy.

- I am not behind. I am exactly where I'm meant to be.
- I trust the process, even when I cannot see the outcome.
- I release who I was to make space for who I am becoming.
- I am committed to my growth, not perfection.
- I honor my voice, my values, and my vision.
- I am resilient, radiant, and rooted in purpose.
- I carry wisdom from every chapter I've lived.
- I am the author of my next chapter. I choose boldness, peace, and truth.
- I am taking a bold step toward my dreams today. I am ready, I am worthy, I am aligned.

This journey is yours, and no one can take it from you. You've done the work. You've shown up. And now, the rest of the story is waiting to be lived. Go forward. Not perfectly but powerfully. Because the world needs what only *you* can bring.

Notes

Chapter 1: My Current Self vs. My Future Self
1. Sonia Sotomayor, *Justice Sonia Sotomayor*, interview by M. Elizabeth Magill, Commonwealth Club of California, January 28, 2013, https://www.commonwealthclub.org/events/archive/transcript/justice-sonia-sotomayor.
2. Dean Graziosi website, "7 Levels Deep Exercise," last accessed April 23, 2025, https://www.deangraziosi.com/wp-content/uploads/2021/03/7-Levels-Deep-Exercise.pdf.

Chapter 2: Clear the Air
1. Amandine S'iita, "How to Manifest Your Destiny," *Medium*, January 22, 2020, https://medium.com/@lagulbranson/how-to-manifest-your-destiny-a1706bdd733f.

Chapter 5: The Power of Proximity
1. Michelle Ferrigno Warren, *The Power of Proximity*, (IVP July 25, 2017).

About the Authors

♦
MEET CHRISTINA VERA

Christina Vera is a passionate leader, speaker, and strategist with over fifteen years of experience in nonprofit management and small business development. Known for her heart-centered approach to leadership, she has designed and facilitated transformative workshops, trainings, and coaching sessions focused on life mapping, career transitions, financial empowerment, and entrepreneurship. Her work is rooted in service, and she is deeply committed to helping others unlock their potential and walk boldly in their purpose.

As the co-founder and associate executive director for Femergy®, Christina is devoted to empowering women and girls through innovative strategies, effective communication, and team development. Her leadership is rooted in a commitment to fostering growth, driving positive change, and building organizational capacity. Her extensive experience spans organizational leadership, project management, and creating sustainable solutions that uplift communities. She also co-founded True Print for Business, a social enterprise specializing in organizational structure, training, and sustainable growth strategies.

As a proud elected official, Christina is serving her first term in Columbus, Ohio, on the Columbus Board of Education after being elected in 2021. In 2024 Christina became the first Latina president in the district's history. Her deep roots in the community and unwavering commitment to public education and equitable access for all drive her dedication to creating meaningful change for youth and families.

When she's not leading or serving, Christina co-hosts the *True Print for Life* podcast, sharing insights and stories to inspire others. At home, she finds joy in spending time with her husband and their three children.

For Christina, leadership isn't just a role; it's a mission. It's about making a difference, creating meaningful impact, meeting people where they are, and helping them amplify the visions and gifts they already possess. Step by step, one bite at a time, she is committed to empowering others to realize their fullest potential.

MEET MAYLIN SAMBOIS

Maylin Sambois is a visionary leader and advocate dedicated to empowering women and girls through education, leadership, service, health, and wellness. As the co-founder and executive director of Femergy®, she has developed and led holistic programs that foster personal and professional growth, equipping individuals with the tools needed to thrive and create meaningful change in their communities. Under her co-leadership, Femergy® has become a powerful force for transformation, reaching countless girls and women with its impactful initiatives.

In addition to her work at Femergy®, Maylin serves as the national director of service reception for La Jornada at the National Youth Advocate Program (NYAP) where she oversees national intake operations and ensures that unaccompanied youth receive compassionate and timely care. She also co-founded True

About the Authors

Print for Business, a social enterprise specializing in organizational structure, training, and sustainable growth strategies. As the co-host of the *True Print for Life* podcast, Maylin shares her passion for mentorship by offering listeners practical insights into strategy, purpose, and personal development.

Born in the Dominican Republic, Maylin moved to New York City in 1994 where she learned firsthand the challenges and opportunities of adapting to a new culture. Early on, she committed herself to service and advocacy, volunteering in hospitals to mentor children struggling with mental health issues. By 2002, she became a counselor, guiding patients transitioning from medical facilities to independent living. These experiences shaped her deep understanding of human resilience and the power of community-driven change.

With over fifteen years of experience, Maylin has designed and facilitated workshops, trainings, and coaching sessions focused on life mapping, career transitions, financial empowerment, health advocacy, and entrepreneurship. She has held leadership roles in small business development, corporate diversity initiatives, and youth programming, including serving as the director of The Latino Small Business Development Center and co-chair of Adelante Ohio. Her unwavering commitment to mentorship and advocacy has impacted countless lives, particularly among young girls and women seeking guidance and support.

Maylin holds a B.A. in Psychology with a minor in Business Administration from St. John's University and a certificate in Public and Nonprofit Leadership from Ohio State University. Outside of her professional life, she is a devoted mother and servant leader who finds joy in reading, dancing, traveling, and giving back to her community. With a heart for service and a vision for change, Maylin continues to inspire and uplift others through her dedication to equity and empowerment.

This may be the last page, but it doesn't have to be the end of our connection. Join the community at https://trueprintforlife.com and let's grow together.

To learn more about Femergy®, please visit www.femergy.org.

If you'd like to connect with Christina or Maylin for coaching or strategy-building support, and to access our free online resources, reach out to us at info@trueprintforlife.com with "The Journey" in the subject line.

We are excited to connect with you!

Christina and *Maylin*

www.ingramcontent.com/pod-product-compliance
Lightning Source LLC
Chambersburg PA
CBHW072046160426
43197CB00014B/2645